+IMPRIMA
BY THE MOST R~~EVEREND~~
FREDERICK F. CAMPBELL,
BISHOP OF COLUMBUS

"The timing for this marvelous book couldn't be better. Elizabeth has given Catholics a real gift as we enter into the Year of Faith and do what we can to help the Church's efforts in the new evangelization. *Seven from Heaven* is an example of what Pope Benedict is asking of all believers: to understand our faith more deeply and to proclaim it more effectively from the housetops. The more we know about the Sacraments the more we can all grow in our faith and help others on their journey to heaven. This book is a great resource that can make a real difference in achieving these spiritual goals."

— Teresa Tomeo, syndicated talk show host
and bestselling Catholic author

"In *Seven from Heaven*, Elizabeth Ficocelli taps into her experience and wisdom and shares it in a book that's equal parts guide and reference. Reading it is like having a good friend give you tips, and families are sure to find the ideas within it indispensable and inspiring."

— Sarah Reinhard, author of SnoringScholar.com and
Welcome Risen Jesus: Lenten & Easter Reflections for Families

"The sacraments are God's gift to us in order to grow closer to Him; however, many individuals fail to fully appreciate the beauty of the sacraments. Elizabeth Ficocelli provides a powerful, practical guide on how to better integrate the sacraments into family life. *Seven from Heaven* demonstrates how the sacraments can help families grow closer to each other, their community, and God."

— Katherine Becker, *The Dating Fast*

"The sacraments are such wonderful gifts! *Seven from Heaven* will help foster or renew your enthusiasm for them. What makes *Seven from Heaven* truly valuable and unique are the ways Elizabeth

Ficocelli suggests to make the sacraments come alive for children. Children, as much as adults, are prone to asking 'What is in it for me?' When it comes to the sacraments, the answer is 'everything!' It is a Catholic parent's job to help their children understand the beauty and blessings of these gifts from God. With her practical suggestions, Ficocelli helps make that job much easier."

—Patrice Fagnant-MacArthur

"An outstanding, practical guide for every Catholic parent! Use *Seven from Heaven* to give your children the greatest gift of all—joyful participation in Christ's presence every day."

—Matthew Kelly, *New York Times* bestselling author

"Now more than ever, Catholic families need support and encouragement for the tremendous task of bringing the Faith to life in the hearts and souls of their children. With inspired advice on everything from navigating the Cry Room to contemplating the commitment of Confirmation with our teens and beyond, Elizabeth Ficocelli's *Seven from Heaven* is the perfect resource for busy parents and teachers who endeavor to instill a love for Christ and His Church with their families, students and parish communities. This book belongs on every parent's kitchen table, on every catechist's desk and in every pastor's library."

—Lisa M. Hendey, Founder and Editor of www.CatholicMom.com and author of *A Book of Saints for Catholic Moms*

"Absolutely outstanding! Elizabeth shines light on the essential elements of our Catholic faith, the sacraments, and equips us to more fully integrate them into our family lives. In the pages of this wonderful book, the transformative power of the sacraments is described in practical, relatable terms. A must read for all Catholics family members who need the healing, nurturing and protection the sacraments provide!"

—Kevin Lowry, husband and father of eight, and author of *Faith at Work: Finding Purpose Beyond the Paycheck*

SEVEN FROM HEAVEN

How Your Family Can Find Healing, Strength, and Protection in the Sacraments

ELIZABETH FICOCELLI

A Crossroad Book
The Crossroad Publishing Company
New York

The Crossroad Publishing Company
www.CrossroadPublishing.com

In continuation of our 200-year tradition of independent publishing, The Crossroad Publishing Company proudly offers a variety of books with strong, original voices and diverse perspectives. The viewpoints expressed in our books are not necessarily those of The Crossroad Publishing Company, any of its imprints or of its employees. No claims are made or responsibility assumed for any health or other benefit.

Printed in the United States of America.

The text of this book is set in Apollo
The display face is Helvetica

Project Management by
The Crossroad Publishing Company
John Jones
For this edition numerous people have shared their talents and ideas, and we gratefully acknowledge Elizabeth Ficocelli, who has been most gracious during the course of our cooperation. We thank especially:

Cover design: Stefan Killen   Text design: WebFusion
Proofreading: Sylke Jackson   Printing: Versa Press

Message development, text development, package, and market
positioning by The Crossroad Publishing Company

Library of Congress Cataloging-in-Publication Data available from the publisher
ISBN 13: 978-0-8245-27075

Books published by The Crossroad Publishing Company may be purchased at special quantity discount rates for classes and institutional use. For information, please e-mail info@CrossroadPublishing.com

CONTENTS

DEDICATION

In loving memory of Caroline Schermerhorn
Wife, mother, homeschooler,
writer, prayer warrior, friend

PREFACE

An Undiscovered Treasure

The first time I was invited to speak professionally as an author, I was terrified. At the time, I had two books under my belt: *Child's Guide to First Holy Communion* and *Child's Guide to Reconciliation*. So it seemed logical to me to address these particular sacraments in my presentation. My dilemma was that my audience would consist of Catholic educators, and I had no previous classroom teaching experience. I had never attended Catholic school; in fact, I was not even raised in the Catholic faith. As an adult convert and a stay-at-home mother of four, I felt woefully inadequate to give an audience of learned women and men (both lay and religious) material that would be new and helpful in their roles as educators in the faith.

For weeks I agonized over how to create a simple paragraph for the conference organizers that would describe the topic of my proposed talk. Then one day, through the mercy of God, I had the inspiration to jot down a list of things my husband and I had been doing at home with our own four boys to make the sacraments of Holy Communion and Reconciliation come alive for them. The list surprised me in terms of its length and creativity. This discovery motivated me to identify other activities and traditions we had incorporated into our family to teach the faith to our children, and I began to see a pattern emerge. Many of these ideas, whether they were our own original creations or ones we had borrowed from other families, tied directly into one of the seven sacraments. I felt a growing excitement as the clouds of doubt dissipated and my mission became focused. I would speak on a broader topic: a family approach to *all seven* sacraments.

The presentation turned out to be a success. By their questions and positive feedback afterward, I could tell that the material had captured the audience's attention and imagination. Of all the presentations I've given through the years, this family approach to the seven sacraments is still one of the most requested by teachers and families. People seem eager for ideas on how to excite young people about their faith, and the seven sacraments are the perfect catechetical tool for doing so. That's because the sacraments are not just something you learn from a book—they are something to *experience*. They are alive. They are living encounters with the Risen Christ and therefore have the power to transform us completely and do the unthinkable in our lives.

Claiming the Gift

In my encounters with Catholics young and not so young, I've discovered a general lack of understanding, appreciation, and enthusiasm when it comes to the sacraments. Many Catholics today have a hard time just remembering the names of the seven sacraments, let alone their meaning and potential impact on their lives. Some people tell me they learned about the sacraments in religion class, but like many school subjects, they retained the information only long enough to regurgitate it on a test. Some older Catholics I've spoken with seem better able to rattle off the names of the sacraments. But once I begin asking them more questions, their answers are less confident—they aren't sure what the sacraments have to do with *their own lives*. For so many people, the sacraments have failed to come alive—their purpose and power remaining forgotten and untapped. It is my hope with this book to reawaken God's gift of the sacraments in individuals and, even more importantly, to families.

I myself knew nothing of the seven sacraments of the Catholic Church until well after my conversion in 1983. From the perspective of a new convert, the sacraments seemed to be just one more part of the mysterious tapestry that made up my new faith. My nominal Protestant formation did little to prepare me for the Catholic understanding of these unique gifts from God. While the sacraments must have been covered in my abbreviated RCIA instruction, I recall very little about them. I was still fairly young, preoccupied with the Catholic man I was about to marry, and overwhelmed with all the newness and vastness of the faith I was about to embrace. Fortunately, God was patient and understanding and would reveal his seven gifts one by one, in his own good time.

I remember as a new Catholic devouring book after book about my newly adopted faith. The first books that drew my attention focused on the supernatural wonders of Catholicism, such as Eucharistic miracles, incorrupt bodies, stigmata, and apparitions. These subjects were completely foreign to me, and I found them exciting and extraordinary. In a quieter but far deeper way, the sacraments would slowly make their way into my consciousness in daily, ordinary living. This was where

I would experience God most poignantly. The sacraments would be a source of great joy for me—and at times a great challenge (as I explain in Chapter 2 on Reconciliation). It would take many years, however, before I was able to recognize the many connections between the seven sacraments—a family nature, if you will—and how they are a blueprint of God's special involvement and protection in our lives from birth until death. My enthusiasm in this discovery would lead to the development of creative activities our whole family could engage in to enable each of us to experience God's special presence throughout our lives, appreciate our faith, and embrace it as our own.

I hope you will find my enthusiasm for the sacraments contagious, and that the ideas shared on the following pages will inspire you at home—and in your classrooms, if you are blessed to be a teacher or catechist—as you live out your special role of handing on the faith to the next generation, our future Church.

INTRODUCTION: THE SEVEN SACRAMENTS

God's Special Protection from Birth until Death

Jesus Christ instituted the seven sacraments to draw us close to his heart, to nourish and heal us in our spiritual journeys, and to properly equip us to do his good work on earth. Jesus knew the struggles, temptations, and potential falls that would await each of us, so he gave us the gift of the sacraments as strategic, spiritual sources of grace to help us reach our destination—heaven and eternal union with him—safely and assuredly. The sacraments are God's powerful presence all around us, touching all the stages and important moments of Christian life. They give us a share in the divine life and help us to grow in holiness.

In my writing and speaking ministry, there is no greater joy than pointing people in the direction of Christ in the sacraments, allowing him to do his work because it is *him* they will encounter there. This is the single most important fact about the sacraments that has been lost on many Catholics today: *the seven sacraments are intimate encounters with the living Christ.* They are God's chosen channels of grace in which the Holy Spirit nourishes and empowers us. They are the tools God employs to help us grow into the people he needs in his Church today. Quite simply, if we're not receiving the sacraments regularly and worthily, we will be hard-pressed to fully and effectively accomplish the work he has planned for us.

The Answers to Life's Difficulties

God's powerful presence in the seven sacraments is the reason they hold the answers to every problem faced today by family and society. His presence is how they can inspire conversions of heart and complete reversals of impossible situations—because with God, all things are possible. All we have to do is get out of the way and let God be God. We can trust God to work in us and in others we may bring to him in the sacraments. This message was communicated effectively on a sign outside a Christian church in my hometown that read, "Be ye fishers of men. You catch 'em, *God* will clean 'em!"

The question is, how do we do this? How do we "catch" people? How do we inspire a shift of mindset, so that our Catholic faith changes from seeming like a small and sometimes inconvenient part of our lives to an essential, joyful part of who we are? One way I've found to help people begin to start shifting is to address the proverbial question: *What's in it for me?* No one would dispute the fact that people today are enormously busy. Especially in a world where so many people struggle with financial burdens and greater demands on their time, they are stretched to the breaking point. They need valid and persuasive reasons why they should invest one more ounce of time and energy in something when their plate is already filled.

The good news is, when it comes to the seven sacraments, the answer to *What's in it for me?* can be summed up in one word: *Everything!*

Let's begin by taking a look at the world we live in. These are pretty serious times, spiritually speaking. The world is full of distractions and temptations that effectively vie for people's attention at every juncture. We are seduced constantly with the allure of materialism and consumerism, and our lives are saturated 24/7 with entertainment and noise. There have been great strides taken in our country to remove God's name and presence from our schools, government offices, and public places. Many people are not raised with any religion at all. With those who were, it has become fashionable for them to forget their religious upbringing and turn their backs on God in order to pursue their own pleasures and worldly interests, without giving much heed to the long-term consequences. These pursuits inevitably end up as disappointments because they are not grounded in truth. Worse, the distorted and self-centered priorities of our culture and the growing lack of God are combining to produce skyrocketing societal ills such as divorce, teen suicide, porn addiction, depression, abortion, and child abuse. The bottom line is that, like the world itself, the things of the world and the satisfaction they offer are passing. Only the knowledge and love of God and the search for ways to serve in his name will bring true and lasting happiness and peace.

Sacraments are the key to turning our lives back to God and stopping the downward spiral that is taking families and society with it. They are the means to invite God into our hearts and *keep* him there. They are the answer to fortifying the family against the evils that want to tear it apart, and the way to keep its members healthy and balanced and unified. And, since the family is a mini-Church and a microcosm of society (more about this topic later), sacraments have the power to transform not only the family but the entire world. If I were to summarize the sacraments in two words, I would say they are all about *love* and *community*. These are not just warm, fuzzy words. Love and community are desperately needed in our families and society today—they are absolutely critical for our survival.

The Power of Love

As human beings, we have been made by God to love and to be loved. We know that God loves us very much. In fact, he loves us unconditionally. He is, after all, perfect love. All God desires is for us to love him back in our imperfect, human way. Therefore, he has created the sacraments as a means to reveal himself and show us his great love for us. He wants to have this exchange of love with us in a special and intimate way. It is through this love exchange with our Creator that we begin to develop a personal relationship with Jesus Christ. The expression "personal relationship with Jesus" can bring about negative connotations in the minds of some Catholics. It sounds too—well, *Protestant*. But our Protestant brothers and sisters have it right when they talk about the necessity of a personal relationship with Jesus. We as Catholics must strive for that, too, as it is exactly this vibrant personal relationship that will make our faith come alive so that we can fully embrace it and hand it on to our children.

One of the best resources I've found for developing a personal relationship with Jesus is the book, *The Imitation of Christ,* by Thomas à Kempis. I was amazed to discover that this Christian classic is the second most widely read book in Christian literature, after the Bible itself. While it continues to be used in the formation process for the priesthood and religious life, only a small fraction of lay Catholics today are familiar with its teachings. Although the book was written over 500 years ago, its messages still apply because its wisdom is derived from Holy Scripture, which of course is timeless. If you are unfamiliar with the book, it is a four-part journey in developing a personal relationship with Jesus. The process consists of making Jesus our true leader, learning how to be better followers, drawing closer to him by developing our spirituality, and finally, consummating our relationship with Christ in the most intimate way possible in this earthly life—through the Eucharist (which, by no coincidence, is one of the seven sacraments!).

It is remarkable how easily the messages of this classic apply to a young audience in modern times. My book *The Imitation of Christ for Children* can be a valuable resource in helping young people today develop this personal love relationship with Jesus. Taking its cue from Thomas à Kempis, it presents in a kid-friendly manner why Jesus is the perfect leader and why it's so essential to follow his lead versus all the others that might be presented to young people today. It takes young readers on the same spiritual journey as the classic takes adults: learning to speak to and listen to God; discovering the joy of putting Jesus first; understanding how our most important goal in life should be getting to heaven; dealing with temptations; and seeking

God's strength from the sacraments. In this process, Jesus goes from being a stranger to a friend, from a friend to a best friend, and from best friend to *beloved*, as we experience the powerful intimacy of the Eucharist.

The Power of Community

As Thomas à Kempis wisely pointed out in his masterpiece, a personal relationship with Christ involves more than just "Jesus and me." It involves community. In fact, it *requires* community. Remember how Jesus taught that the Ten Commandments could be summarized in the first two: to love God and to love one another? We as Christians are called to be loving people in community. The seven sacraments are all about building that community, with God at the center.

Let me illustrate. In the Sacrament of Baptism, a new member joins the parish community and that community is forever changed. In the Sacrament of Reconciliation, a person is reconciled to God, the Church, *and* the community after being separated by sin. In the Sacrament of the Eucharist, we share a holy meal with a parish community and are united in that sharing. But "community" is even wider than the parish. In the Sacrament of Confirmation, we are called to witness and evangelize to the greater community, the world. Likewise, in the Sacrament of Matrimony a couple is called to reflect God's love to the community. In the Sacrament of Holy Orders, individuals come forth to serve the community. And finally, in the Sacrament of the Anointing of the Sick, a person is reconciled to the community (through the sacrament's nature to forgive sins) and in some cases, is prepared to join the greatest community of all: the community of heaven. As you can see, sacraments are all about community. They provide *personal* strengthening, yes, but always in conjunction with our relationships with one another.

Society, on the other hand, cares little about people being in community. Our culture conditions us to be me-centered and ignore how our personal decisions may affect the community at large. This mindset is deeply ingrained and admittedly challenging to change. We live in a world of illusion, or perhaps more accurately, *delusion*. We have a false sense of reality, shaped by what we see and hear in the media. We work frantically at keeping our outsides looking good with plastic surgery, the right clothing, and fancy cars so that no one can see what's going on *inside*. No longer real to ourselves or with one another, we begin to feel isolated and lonely in our relationships. We begin to think everyone else must have it together *except* us. This is why disasters happen within family life, to ordinary families just like yours and mine. The truth is, we are all broken people. We may know this intellectually, but emotionally we are still hesitant to seek support from the community, whether it be our church, our neighborhood, or at times even our own family. Who is behind this division? The evil one. He wants us to keep our suffering in the darkness. He knows that when we are isolated in our weakness we become all the more vulnerable to his attacks. Jesus, on the other hand, wants us to bring our sufferings to the light and seek support and friendship from others. He knows we are stronger when we are united—when we are *community*.

One of the most compelling examples of the importance of community—and the devastation that can result when this community is threatened—is discussed in George Weigel's book *Witness to Hope: The Biography of Pope John Paul II*. The book is a fascinating chronicle of a man of extraordinary holiness and his powerful effect on the world during his 26-year pontificate. There are dozens of good reasons to read the book, but one paragraph in particular has had a profound effect on me. Mr. Weigel was describing the conditions in the late pope's homeland of Poland, when the communist regime took control of the nation specifically by breaking down and controlling family life:

> Perhaps the hardest-fought battle between Church and regime involved family life, for the communists understood that men and women secure in the love of their families were a danger. Housing, work schedules, and school hours were all organized by the state to separate parents from their children as frequently as possible. Apartments were constructed to accommodate only small families, so that children would be regarded as problems. Work was organized in four shifts and families were rarely together. The workday began at 6 or 7 a.m. so children had to be consigned to state-run child-care centers before school. The schools themselves were consolidated, and children were moved out of their local communities for schooling. A permissive law was passed that regarded abortion as a means of birth control... (pg. 97, Witness to Hope)

What struck me most about the sinister plan of the communists to manipulate Poland is how closely it resembles our own contemporary culture. The crucial difference is, we *willingly* live in division and give our freedoms away, weakening our families and society and enslaving ourselves in the process. Privacy acts, moral relativism, busy schedules, and isolation from our neighbors all contribute to keeping us from being in community and set us up for failure. The seven sacraments are God's way of uniting his children in community with him and with one another.

Our Role in the Sacraments

Our role in the sacraments is to understand them, prepare for them, and participate in them. The more we participate in the sacraments, the more our desire increases for them, and the more our relationship with God begins to deepen.

The Catholic Church groups the sacraments into three categories: *The Sacraments of Christian Initiation* (Baptism, Confirmation, and Holy Eucharist), *The Sacraments of Healing* (Reconciliation and the Anointing of the Sick), and *The Sacraments at the Service of Communion* (Sacraments of Matrimony and Holy Orders). Baptism, Confirmation, and the Eucharist lay the foundations of every Christian life. They confer on each of us a common vocation as a disciple of Christ—a vocation to holiness and to the mission of evangelizing the world. Reconciliation and the Anointing of the Sick help protect our new life in Christ from being weakened by and even entirely lost to sin. Marriage and Holy Orders confer a particular mission on certain individuals to serve others and build up the people of God. For the purposes of this book, rather than presenting the traditional grouping of the sacraments, I am going to present them in the order that a person would typically experience them in life. This can remind us of the way that the sacraments nourish us and our families from birth to death.

With that in mind, let's begin with the Sacrament of Baptism.

1

IMMERSED IN GRACE

The Sacrament of Baptism

Like many of us, I have no memory of my own baptism. A few photos and a small certificate produced by the Lutheran church of my childhood are the only proof that I received the sacrament. At the time I had no say whatsoever in the matter; I was baptized solely on my parents' faith and commitment. Yet this simple ritual involving water and prayer would change my life forever. As if to emphasize its significance, the Catholic Church recognized my infant baptism as valid when I sought full communion with the Church as a young adult. Therefore, there was no need to repeat the sacrament.

What Catholic Baptism Means

According to the Catechism of the Catholic Church, "Holy Baptism is the basis of the whole Christian life, the gateway to life in the Spirit, and the door that gives access to the other sacraments. Through Baptism we are freed from sin and reborn as sons of God; we become members of Christ, are incorporated into the Church, and made sharers in her mission." (1213)

Jesus instituted the Sacrament of Baptism when he commissioned his twelve apostles to make disciples of all nations, baptizing them in the name of the Father, the Son, and the Holy Spirit. He told us it is necessary for our salvation when he said, "Truly, truly, I say to you, unless one is born of water and the Spirit, he cannot enter the Kingdom of God."(John 3:5, RSV) In gratitude for this priceless gift of salvation, the Church baptizes infants as young as a few days or weeks old (or, if there is some medical danger, even as soon as they are born.) The word *baptism* comes from the Greek and means to "plunge" or "immerse." We are "plunged" into the water three times, symbolizing the death of ourselves (and our sins) being united with the death and burial of Christ, and our resurrection with him as a new creation. The washing with water is therefore a sign of purification and renewal. We believe as Catholics that all of our sins are forgiven in baptism—both original sin and those that we have voluntarily committed. Through God's grace, the punishment from these sins is also pardoned. (This doesn't mean that people are preserved from committing sins and risking their salvation in the future. That's why Christ instituted the Sacrament of Reconciliation, the subject of the next chapter.) Baptism leaves an indelible mark on the soul of the baptized, which is why valid baptisms are never repeated.

Baptism is not a "cute" ritual or something we do out of a desire to please an elderly relative who has old-fashioned beliefs. It is a serious and grace-filled sacrament that is empowering and life-changing, and one we want to seek with heartfelt desire. Parents who undertake the responsibility of baptizing their child in the Catholic church need to fully understand the commitment they are making—that is, to raise the child in the Catholic faith. For this reason, before approaching the baptismal font with their children, it is customary for parents to receive proper sacramental preparation.

Baptism Class

Most parishes today offer a baptism class for parents preparing to have a child baptized. This is an excellent opportunity to connect with other young families and meet some of the spiritual leaders of the parish. An effective baptism class is warm and welcoming to its families. It conveys the message that these families are important to the community and that their presence at Mass is greatly desired. Hopefully, the baptism class experience will mark the beginning of a long, active, and happy life in the parish.

The baptism class is a perfect opportunity for new parents to think about their own relationship with God and the Church. Sometimes one of the parents who are baptizing a child may not be Catholic and may feel uncomfortable about the process. Others who are Catholic may have misunderstandings and misperceptions about their faith. The baptism class provides a safe and supportive environment to bring up questions and concerns in order to receive clear explanations of what the Church teaches. Just as importantly, the baptism class teaches families about the serious nature of the commitment parents are about to make in baptizing their child in the Catholic Church and raising that child in the faith. This commitment includes bringing that child to Mass on Sunday and preparing him or her to receive the sacraments.

A common misunderstanding about baptism is that it is a private family affair. In the Catholic Church, nothing could be further from the truth. Through the Sacrament of Baptism, a bond of unity is formed with one another, because we are incorporated into Christ and his Church. Therefore, every time an individual enters the Church through baptism, the parish community is directly affected. That's why baptisms usually take place during (or immediately following) the Mass. It's a community celebration!

Baptism Preparation Activities

A number of activities can help in the preparation process for the Sacrament of Baptism. Here are several to consider.

Pray with Your Spouse

The most important advice I can offer new parents or parents-to-be is to start praying together as a couple. Prayer is a powerful tool that is mentioned frequently in this book because it works, and there is nothing more powerful than family prayer. Many older Catholics were raised in families that prayed rosaries or other prayers together. While unfortunately this tradition seems to have fallen to the wayside, I'm pleased to see it gradually making a comeback.

The start of a new family is a wonderful time for couples to begin praying together, but no matter what stage a family is in, it is never too late to incorporate a regimen of prayer. For many husbands and wives, praying together will seem awkward at first—it can actually be more of an intimate and vulnerable experience than making love. With practice and patience, however, praying together as a couple will become more natural, and couples will be surprised at how it strengthens their union. Couples can pray for themselves as parents or prospective parents, and they can also pray for their child—even (and especially) before he or she is born. Starting family prayer when children are young can be tremendously bonding and will become second nature for the parents as their children grow older and need the parents' prayers all the more. Prayer works wonders—never underestimate this powerful gift!

Write a Letter to Your Baby

Another activity I suggest for parents is to write a letter to their baby, sharing their hopes and dreams for that child as he or she grows to follow God. This exercise gives parents an opportunity to sort out these thoughts in their own heads and share some of those ideas with their spouse. Crafting such a letter can help unify the couple and also serve as a commitment in writing for the couple to encourage them to make it a priority to raise their little one as a child of God.

Choose the Right Baptismal Name

The discernment of a baptismal name is one that can yield surprising fruits. Even though it's popular today for people to name their children after states or movie stars or words that sound pleasing to the ear, we as Catholics have a wonderful tradition of naming our children after great saints who have gone before us. We'll discuss saints in Chapter 4 on

Confirmation, but for now I will say that the saints are one of our Church's great treasures that can truly help us grow in holiness. Saints are men, women, and sometimes children whom the Church has raised up for our example because all of us are called to be saints. My husband and I wanted all the help we could get in raising our children, so when it came to naming them, we figured we would cover the bases: we named them after an archangel, a bishop, a prophet, and an Apostle. I've found it interesting that as our boys grow, their personalities seem to match the holy ones for whom they were named. Michael Thomas, for example, is a warrior for the faith. He defends Catholicism among his peers, and he's a great leader and protector of his younger brothers. At the same time, he's quite the thinker and questions *everything*. Nicholas Joseph tends to be kind and gentle and generous. Our younger ones are still growing into their personalities, but already I have seen Daniel Vincent demonstrate tenacity and bravery. He also has a soft spot for the less fortunate. Matthew David was named because he was a "gift from God" as his first name implies, and not our own idea. Like David, he is also the youngest of his brothers with a natural ability to lead. (He prefers Nerf® guns to slingshots, however!)

Choose Appropriate Godparents

Another decision we must discern in preparation for baptism is the choice of godparents. In the Catholic Church, godparents are not figureheads but vital links between the family and the Church—a tangible example of that connection to community we talked about earlier. It is the responsibility of the godparents to see that godchildren are raised in the faith and *remain* in the faith. Therefore, godparents should be practicing Catholics with a good knowledge of the tenets of our faith and an earnest desire to play a vital role in the child's sacramental journey. If a godparent lives far away, there are still plenty of communication technologies available today to stay connected. (Just ask the godchild!) The bond between godparent and godchild is meant to last a lifetime, just like the Sacrament of Baptism.

Attend Easter Vigil

A terrific way to foster a deeper appreciation of baptism is to attend the Easter Vigil, the Church's formal celebration of this sacrament. If you've never experienced it, the Easter Vigil is one of the most beautiful celebrations of the liturgical year. It begins with the lighting and blessing of a small fire outside of the parish building, symbolizing the light that Christ brings to a world darkened with sin. The Easter candle is lit from this fire and brought into the darkened sanctuary. Candles held by parishioners are lit from this one light, and the room begins to illuminate as the light of Christ is spread from person to person. Biblical accounts of salvation history are sung or read, as the lights of the church are gradually turned up. Other rituals include the blessing of the baptismal water and the Easter candle. But the climax of the Easter Vigil is the formal acceptance into the Church of those adults and young people who have been preparing for this night for nine months. It truly brings alive the meaning of baptism and makes a person proud to be a part of this glorious faith.

Educational Opportunities for Baptism

In order for the graces of this sacrament to unfold, the baptized child or adult will need his or her faith nurtured through the help of parents, godparents, and others. A child's first impressions and experiences of faith and God come primarily through us as parents, which is both a privilege and an awesome responsibility. As children get older, there are opportunities to help them understand what the Sacrament of Baptism means in their lives.

Teach Them Why

For starters, children have a right to know why they were baptized—and why they were baptized *Catholic*. Although it is in vogue today in our culture to be tolerant of everyone, no matter what their beliefs, we as Catholics do not have to lose sight of the fact that we have something unique and special. It's okay to be comfortable in the knowledge that we have the fullness of the truth. This is not to negate the existence of other religions. It is simply to acknowledge that the Catholic Church was founded by Jesus Christ 2000 years ago. We have preserved his teaching through Holy Scripture and Tradition and through an unbroken line of apostolic succession all the way back to Peter, whom Jesus appointed as the first head of the Church. These solid reasons are why we have chosen the Catholic faith for our child, and why we are enthusiastic about sharing what we have with others.

One of our jobs as parents is to raise our children with the understanding that they are loved and special in our eyes *and* in the eyes of God. Our children need this sense of belonging and protection more than ever, due to the times we live it. Let them know that through baptism, they have become a child of God forever. No one and no circumstance— even death—can take that away from them.

Read Bible Stories about Baptism

An effective way to teach children about baptism is to share stories with them from the Bible that prefigure this sacrament. For example, read together the story of creation from Genesis and how the Spirit of God breathed its holiness on the waters. They'll probably already be familiar with the story of Noah and the ark, but you can draw out its relevance to the Sacrament of Baptism by emphasizing how the waters of the great flood were like the waters of baptism in that they saved Noah and his family, giving them new life. At the same time, the waters brought about death, which alludes to the death of our sins and the death Christ endured on the cross for our salvation.

Another famous "water" story from Holy Scripture is the crossing of the Red Sea. To free Moses and his fellow Israelites from their captivity in Egypt, God parted the waters so that the Israelites could cross safely without drowning (which was the unfortunate fate for Pharaoh's soldiers). This liberation from slavery prefigures the liberation from sin and death that happens through the Sacrament of Baptism. A second miracle involving water occurs in the crossing of the Jordan River. This time we find the Israelites in the midst of wandering around the desert for forty years. They arrive at the Jordan River, but its depth prevents them from crossing

over to the Promised Land. God instructs Joshua to have
the Ark of the Covenant carried down to the water's edge,
and once again, the waters part to permit safe crossing. The
Promised Land in this story can be likened to the promise of
eternal life we receive as adopted children of God through
the Sacrament of Baptism.

Certainly, Jesus' own baptism by John in the same Jordan
River is an important teaching tool for our children. Jesus
willingly subjected himself to a baptism meant for sinners,
though he himself was sinless. In emptying himself in this
manner, he was filled with the Holy Spirit who hovered
above the waters at that sacred moment in the form of a
dove. The Father identifies Jesus as his "beloved Son" (Matt
3:16–17), and the Savior's mission begins. This mission will
culminate in Jesus' sacrificial death on the cross. It is on that
cross that we have the greatest prefiguring of baptism. After
the Roman soldier pierced Jesus' heart to ensure that he was
dead, blood and water flowed out. The blood represents the
Eucharist and the water represents baptism—the sacraments
of new life. Jesus' death on the cross makes it possible for us
to be born of water and the Spirit so that we can enter the
Kingdom of God.

Observe Baptisms in Other Families

In addition to teaching children about baptism through the
use of Bible stories, you can explain the sacrament more
fully when you see a family carrying an infant dressed in
white into Mass. Begin by explaining the purpose of the holy
water font at the entrance to the church, which we use to
bless ourselves as a reminder of our baptism and a gesture to

purify ourselves before the presence of God. Point out quietly to your children what is happening during the baptism as Father anoints the baby's crown with chrism oil, declaring that the child shares in Christ's mission as priest, prophet, and king. Make note of the garment of white, symbolizing purity and how we are to "put on Christ" as St. Paul tells us (Galatians 3:27). And explain how we are enlightened through our baptism, which is why the priest presents the parents with a lighted candle. Encourage your children to renew their baptismal vows with the congregation through an emphatic, "We do!" If possible, sit near the baptismal font so your children have a good view of all the action.

Family Traditions for Baptism

A baptism is a cause for celebration. The entire family should be invited, and older siblings should be encouraged to take part in the occasion. But the celebration doesn't have to be limited to the day the sacrament is received. Families can celebrate the *anniversaries* of their baptisms by marking them in red on the calendar or adding them to their desktop and cell phone calendars. The celebration can be simple, such as lighting the baptismal candle that was given to the child on that special day, looking at photos of the event, and recalling special memories. (Note: only burn the baptism candle briefly so you can repeat this celebration for years to come!)

Catholic author and speaker Dr. Marcellino D'Ambrosio is a father of five. He writes that at his family's baptismal celebrations, the family renews their baptismal vows, with Marcellino asking the questions. The baptismal vow is a powerful series of statements in which we declare our embrace of the faith and our firm rejection of Satan. It's an excellent way to bond and fortify the family.

Baptism and Beyond

The effect of Catholic baptism on family life, when understood and applied correctly, is dynamic. Through this sacrament we are not just members of a family: we are members of the Body of Christ. As such, we no longer belong to ourselves but to Jesus Christ who died and rose for us. Our entire life becomes a call to serve others. Fortunately, the Sacrament of Baptism fully equips us for a life of service because baptism, like all of the sacraments, is a source of grace. Through baptism we are infused with the grace to believe in God, to hope in him, and to love him. The sacrament gives us the ability to discern the promptings of the Holy Spirit and act accordingly. Specifically, through this sacrament we receive the gifts of the Holy Spirit: wisdom, understanding, counsel, fortitude, knowledge, piety, and fear of the Lord. (We'll be talking more about these gifts in Chapter 4 on Confirmation.) At the same time, we are given three other gifts of grace from God: the theological virtues of faith, hope, and charity. With such God-given grace and gifts, we are well-prepared to face the challenges of life!

The Family Mass Survival Guide

Too often, families who have a child baptized in the Catholic Church stop coming to Mass. One of the factors that can keep a family away from church is the inability to deal with behavior problems of an infant or small child. I would like to conclude this chapter on baptism by offering some help and advice in this area. As a parent of four, I understand that it's not always easy to bring young ones to Mass—in fact, at times it's not always easy to bring *older* children! Our family has had our share of crying infants, obstinate toddlers, busy middle school children, and distracted teenagers. For many families in this situation, the battle of behavior is not worth the effort of going to Mass together. I could not disagree more. The graces afforded at Mass for the entire family are critical. It is imperative to bring our children with us every week to receive the wisdom of the word and the grace of the Sacrament of the Eucharist. Worshipping together is one of the most important things we can do as a family. I am convinced that it is possible to teach children proper behavior in church, but just like every other discipline, it takes love, time, consistency, and *lots* of patience.

The behavior of children at Mass can be a subject of great controversy in some parishes. The bottom line is, our children deserve to be at Mass. We deserve to be there, too. *And so does every person sitting around us.* As families with youngsters, we must be respectful of the fact that others are in need of God's nourishment too. We are people in community, remember? Therefore, it is our responsibility as parents to try and do everything we can to minimize our children's distractions.

Avoiding Mass Hysteria

On my website (www.elizabethficocelli.com) I have an article called "Avoiding Mass Hysteria: Teaching Children How to Behave in Church."[1] Over the years, the article has been distributed in a number of parishes to offer parents constructive ideas in the area of behavior management in church. The inspiration for the article came one day as I was sitting in Mass with my youngest in my arms. He was about 18 months old at the time. The family sitting directly behind us decided to open a family-size bag of cheese curls, and instantly, my little guy wanted some – a fact he made quite clear to the entire congregation. Immediately, I was on my feet and headed to the back of the church.

In those days, our parish did not have a traditional cry room. We had a room across the vestibule with a small crackly speaker that piped in the Mass. I took my little Matthew in there, who by now had become quite distraught over the fact that he wasn't going to get any cheese curls. I felt frustrated that I had been ousted by what I felt was a ridiculous thing to bring to Mass. As I stood there perturbed, rocking Matthew into quietness so I could take him back to the liturgy, I tried to make out what Father was saying through the static of the speaker. It was particularly hard to hear over the voice of a woman, sitting at my feet, reading the story of Goldilocks and the Three Bears to her children. I looked at her, trying not to make a scene in front of the other families who had set up camp in the room, but the woman went on reading. Finally, I bent down and said to her as politely as possible, "Excuse me, but I can't hear Father." The woman looked up at me blankly before returning to her reading. Now I was no longer feeling charitable. "Excuse me," I said again a bit louder. She looked at me impatiently. I looked at her children, confused by the interruption. "You should be encouraging them to listen to the Mass." Well, that didn't go over too well. The woman gave me a very annoyed "humph!" and read even louder. I left the room with steam coming from my ears. As I marched down the aisle to my seat, past the cheese curl family, I struggled to regain my composure. I was about to serve as Eucharistic Minister, and my heart was full of less-than-Christ-like emotions toward these families. Then, a thought occurred to me that brought me great peace. Why not write an article to help these families? Give them some ideas they can use with their children so that *everyone* can get more out of Mass.

In the article, I share a combination of ideas that my husband and I gleaned from other people, read in a book, or made up ourselves, that have made Mass with four boys a survivable—and even an enjoyable—experience. For example, we've learned that a successful Mass experience begins at home. This is the place we review with our children proper church etiquette—when we stand, sit, kneel, pray, sing, and listen; *why* we sing or pray or make a certain gesture; and what kind of conduct we expect from our children during Mass. On the way to Mass, our family reads the day's readings from the missalette, letting all those who are old enough participate. If time permits, we discuss what we've read. We also allow enough time for a quick potty break before we enter Mass so it won't be an issue during the celebration.

Leave the Food and Toys at Home

A fundamental rule in our family is absolutely no food or toys in church (with the exception of nursing or bottle-feeding an infant). Although families who bring toys and snacks to the liturgy mean well and do so believing it will keep their children quiet, food and toys end up being more of a distraction than the child, both to the family and to everyone else in the neighboring pews. I'm not sure when it started, but it seems to have become an unwritten rule among new Catholic parents that picnic baskets and toy bags are a prerequisite to making it through Mass. (This can quickly get out of hand. I once saw a remote control car and even a full-size basketball enter the sanctuary of my own parish.) If parents don't start the food-and-toys-in-church habit, their children will never miss it. And if they quit bringing these things to Mass, their children will get over it. Here's another bonus: it's one less thing to run around and pack when you are running late for Mass!

Ways to Sit

One of the most successful tips on behavior that our family borrowed from some friends is the rule that until a child turns three years old, his feet never hit the floor in church. The child is carried into the sanctuary and carried out. He sits on a lap and is never allowed to wiggle down and crawl around where it is easy to bang his head against the pew. The child is held lovingly, but firmly, with no exceptions. If he struggles, he is promptly removed. Since this rule, like the others, is discussed at home, the little ones come to accept it rather quickly. The toddler understands that with the advent of his third birthday, he will be entitled to his own seat in church, and he looks forward to that privilege with great anticipation. But this privilege comes with conditions.

The child must sit, stand, and kneel along with the family. If he begins to climb around or abuse his privilege in any way, he becomes a lap-sitter for the remainder of Mass until the next time. This lesson is learned very quickly if you are consistent.

Setting the Right Tone

Where our family sits at Mass often depends on the stage of our youngest child. Sometimes we find that sitting down in front gives our children a lot to see with few distractions. At other times, especially when we've had a rather active youngster, the back of church has made for easier exits when necessary. Often, we find sitting near the choir or the organ is entertaining for little ears. And always, my husband and I try to set the stage for how we feel worship should be. We try to sing joyfully and sway gently to the music when holding youngsters. We respond enthusiastically, carefully speaking the Creed or the Our Father into our child's ear so he can hear every important word. We show reverence during the consecration with a bow of our heads. As our boys have gotten older, we participate in the Mass by bringing up the gifts, serving on the altar, and participating in youth music groups. We find the more we put into Mass, the more we get out of it.

The Cry Room

I've met plenty of disgruntled parishioners who are fed up with Mass being interrupted by the emotional outbursts of small children. They can't wait to have these noisy culprits "under glass" – in other words, placed in the "cry room." At the other end of the argument are families who contend that children have a right to be in church and find it insulting to use the cry room at all, crying baby or no crying baby.

The cry room seems to be a Catholic phenomenon. Most Protestant churches I have visited have nurseries where parents drop their young ones off to play until the worship service is over. I think the idea of a cry room that allows families to hear and see the Mass is a valid one, but I don't think most cry rooms are used appropriately. The cry room was designed to be a temporary place to settle an active child *while still being able to participate in the Mass.* That's why the room typically has a glass window and a speaker. For many people, however, the cry room has become a playroom, a reading room, and a convenient hangout. People can spend the entire hour there and become engrossed in watching the activity going on in the room instead of focusing on and participating in the Mass. This defeats the purpose. To work most effectively, the cry room should only be used when absolutely necessary and be devoid of books, toys, and food. Parents using the cry room should hold their children in their arms and return to Mass as soon as the child is quieted. While there, it is appropriate to listen to and participate in the liturgy, just as though you are sitting in the pews. Of course, there are always going to be exceptional cases with children, for instance, with special needs. This advice is meant for the general populace. Finally, it is wise to use this facility sparingly; excessive use of the cry room delays the process of teaching a child to behave at Mass.

When Mass Is Over, The Learning Doesn't Have to Be

After Mass is over, our family makes it a point to compliment our children on good choices they made during the liturgy. If there was a problem with a child old enough to know better, we ask him to apologize to the people nearby who might have been negatively affected by his choices. This is done without a lot of fanfare to avoid humiliation, but to instill accountability. On the way home, we discuss what happened at Mass. How did God speak to us today? Did we learn something new? Was there something we did not understand? We even use negative experiences as the basis for something positive. Did someone or something cause a distraction during the Mass? How did that make us feel? Even today, some Masses are better experiences than others. But overall, we're a better family for attending together.

Looking Ahead...

What better way to start life than with the Sacrament of Baptism! We've seen how this sacrament frees us from sin and makes us members of Christ and his Church. We've looked at ways to prepare ourselves as we present our children for this special sacrament, and ideas and activities to help our children understand the reason we baptized them Catholic. Through baptism, we have been given a strong footing for life. But what happens if we slip and fall? Will the waters of baptism that washed away our sinfulness be enough for the rest of our journey? We'll answer that question in the next chapter on Reconciliation.

2

FONT OF FORGIVENESS

The Sacrament of Reconciliation

As we saw in the last chapter, the Sacrament of Baptism cleanses us from all sin and gives us a wonderful new beginning. But God knew how easy it would be for his children to fall from grace and jeopardize our salvation through the misuse of our free wills. He knew there would be times when we would give in to temptation and stubbornly turn our hearts away from him, reaping devastating effects on ourselves, the Church, and the world. That's why he instituted another sacrament to serve as a safeguard for us, one to fortify us against evil and bring us a sense of peace and consolation that the world cannot give. This sacrament, known as *Reconciliation* or *Confession*, restores us to God's grace when we have separated ourselves through sin, and joins us with him again in intimate friendship.

Misconceptions

Sadly, the majority of Catholics today miss out on this great gift of God's mercy, because of misconceptions about this sacrament. As a convert to the faith, I had many of these same misconceptions myself.

When I entered the Catholic Church in 1983, my greatest obstacle was not the usual ones that bother so many former Protestants. It wasn't the Eucharist. It wasn't the Blessed Mother. It was the Sacrament of Reconciliation, introduced to me in one ominous word: *Confession.* Being raised in a stoic German family that didn't talk much about feelings or personal matters, I was mortified at the idea of having to go into one of those dark little "closets" in my new Catholic parish and tell my worst sins to a complete stranger. It was only through the miraculous grace of God that I finally came to appreciate the gift and joy of this life-giving sacrament.

In the Lutheran church I attended in my youth, confession of sins was a far less intimidating process. The congregation would stand at a certain point in the worship and, with the pastor, recite a statement of confession that we read out of a book. The pastor would then turn to face the congregation and read a response that essentially told us we were forgiven. Despite the language of the liturgy, I don't remember feeling "heartily sorry" for my sins—or heartily forgiven, for that matter. It was just a routine part of our Sunday ritual.

When I became Catholic, I realized I would have to do confession *the Catholic way*. I dreaded the whole idea, but at the same time I wanted to be obedient to my new faith. So once or twice a year I would drag myself to church to receive the sacrament. I made it a point to avoid going to my own parish, because I was certain that my pastor kept a mental inventory (or worse, a little black book) of everyone's sins and that he would not think very highly of me if he knew how "bad" I was. My faith was not yet strong enough to see beyond the man in the white collar sitting across from me. I couldn't comprehend that it was Jesus and *his* forgiveness that I was encountering in the sacrament. Anxious to get the whole thing over with, I would race through my litany of sins as quickly as possible, and afterward I felt no different. I was so self-focused on how terrible and unforgivable I was that I completely missed the gift of forgiveness.

Miracle of Mercy

Finally, God worked a miracle in my life to help me understand what the Sacrament of Reconciliation was all about. It happened several years ago during Lent, shortly before Easter. I had just finished reading the writings of a young Polish nun, Faustina Kowalska (known today as Saint Faustina) and I was excited about her message of God's Divine Mercy. I was making a Divine Mercy novena at the time and had plans to go to Confession on the Sunday after Easter for a complete pardon of sins, according to the promise Jesus had made to Faustina during her visions.

Inspired to share the story of Divine Mercy with my prayer group, I had located a video on Faustina and put together a little presentation. Just when things were going so well, disaster struck and I committed one of the most regrettable sins of my life. A long string of sleepless nights caring for a newborn baby had been taking a serious toll on my patience level and rational thinking ability. One bleary morning, I lost what was left of my emotional control and raged against my four-year-old in a way that filled me with profound shame and regret. I was devastated and shocked at how such an unbridled outburst could occur during the holiest time of the year. When I regained my composure, I immediately sought forgiveness from my son and my husband. I knew, however, that most importantly I had to reconcile with God. Most of me wondered if I could be forgiven at all.

The following day was Palm Sunday. As the Church prepared for its most holy week of celebration, I felt as if I should be counted among the ranks of Judas and Peter, betrayer and denier. Ashamed and unable to live with myself, I imposed an added penance of going to my own pastor to make my confession. Inside the confessional, it all came out. Between sobs, I told the pastor what I had done. He was very understanding and gave me some advice, and then administered absolution. I still felt terrible and could barely lift myself from my chair.

As I was leaving the confessional, however, a most amazing thing happened. I suddenly experienced an incredible, tangible sensation—as if someone were pouring a bucket of water over my head. I felt washed clean, tingling all the way down to my feet, and feather-light, like the weight of the world had just been lifted off my shoulders. I had never experienced anything like this before. I recognized at once that God was giving me an unmistakably clear sign that I was truly forgiven. He had seen how my heart was breaking and how genuinely contrite I was, and he was happy to welcome me back. His words, as given to Sister Faustina, occurred to me,

> *"I pour out a whole ocean of graces upon those souls who approach the fount of My mercy... all the divine floodgates through which graces flow are opened."*
>
> (*Diary*, 699).

That day, I was privileged to feel the "ocean" of God's mercy poured out for me. For the first time, I truly felt forgiven, and it was a wonderful, freeing feeling. Although I've never experienced that same tangible sensation again, I know that every time I make a good Confession and am truly sorry for my sins, the miracle happens—I am washed clean. Through this same confession, *each of us* is washed clean. If forgiveness from God were always to come as tangibly as I was privileged to experience it that day, I'm sure the lines for Confession would be far longer. But God works signs and wonders in our lives according to our needs. Evidently, on that day, I needed something pretty significant to get my attention. From that experience, I was finally able to learn how to let go of my sins and forgive myself.

Today, when I receive the Sacrament of Reconciliation, I no longer drag my feet, focusing only on my sins. Now, I look forward to receiving God's mercy. I look forward to being unburdened, and feeling close to Our Lord once again. Instead of seeking out priests I don't know, I can now go comfortably to any of the clergy in my own parish. Each priest has his own style, but the absolution is always the same because it comes from God. Through the years, I've developed a special relationship with one of our priests by making him my primary confessor. This way, he's better equipped to help me overcome obstacles in my spiritual growth as I live out my vocation as wife and mother. For me, an adult convert, the Sacrament of Reconciliation has become a way of encountering Christ intimately and meaningfully, second only to receiving him in the Eucharist. At last, I experience Confession the way God has always intended it: as a great gift. Is it harder than my former Lutheran way? Yes. But it's far more rewarding in the long run. It's one of my greatest joys today to speak on the Sacrament of

Reconciliation to audiences of all ages because of the great lesson God has taught me about this sacrament. My story, which was later printed as a magazine article, seems to touch people young and old.[2] Once I had a woman call me who said she had been away from the sacrament for twenty years, but after reading my story, she was going back. When I spoke on the gift of Reconciliation at a women's retreat in northern Ohio recently, the lines for Confession were so long they had to bring in the retired bishop to hear them all. As I was leaving Mass at the end of that retreat, the pastor grabbed my arm. He was as excited as a little kid on Christmas morning. He told me one of the women who came to talk to him that day hadn't been to Confession in *forty years*. Clearly, this is the Holy Spirit at work. People are hungry for the mercy and forgiveness of God. All we have to do is present it to them in a way that invites them to experience it for themselves.

Negative Perceptions about Confession

For those who haven't been privileged to experience God's grace and forgiveness in such a powerful, tangible way, attitudes toward Confession can range from confusion to apathy to downright hostility. I once heard a director of religious education describe Reconciliation as an "orphaned" sacrament, and I think she's right. This is true for many Catholics and especially true for families with young children, where it seems to get overshadowed and forgotten in all the preparations we do for First Holy Communion. But it's a sacrament that shouldn't be forgotten, because it's a very special and powerful gift that can help us for the rest of our lives. "This sacrament," the DRE rightly pointed out, "is the one we should be throwing the party for!"

When I speak with children about Reconciliation, I tell them how Catholics used to go to Confession every week. In those days, it was unheard of to think of receiving Jesus in the Eucharist on Sunday without making a Confession the night before. Children are always surprised to hear this, because that certainly isn't their experience today. I like to share with them a story I once heard about one of those families who used to go to Confession every Saturday night. Saturday was the day when the mother of this family would wash the bed sheets, so when the children came home from church that evening, after they had made their confessions, they would slip into their beds made with freshly washed sheets. The children equated Confession with the feeling of being washed clean and starting the new week fresh and new, just like their bed sheets. I think that's a beautiful image.

Despite some modifications in the past several decades to make the Sacrament of Reconciliation more welcoming to people (such as face-to-face Confession and an emphasis on "reconciliation" versus "penance"), the Sacrament of Reconciliation is still not received with the fervor it could and should be. Simply look at the confessional line at any parish on a late Saturday afternoon. The Church requires Catholics to make a Confession of serious sins at least once a year (Canon 989), but strongly suggests the sacrament be used throughout the year, particularly during Lent and Advent. But for most Catholics, it has probably been a lot longer than that. Why the decline in Confession? What's holding people back from receiving God's forgiveness?

Confusion over Sin

I think the biggest reason for the decline in Confession today is the lack of emphasis and clarity on matters of sin. We live in a culture where moral relativism prevails—in other words, there is no "truth" other than what we personally perceive that truth to be. This mentality makes it convenient to justify any sort of belief or lifestyle choice. As Catholics, we reject the notion of moral relativism. God has given us the truth, whether it fits in comfortably in our lives or not. But society's pervasive mentality has had its effects nonetheless, and religious leaders today seem less willing to challenge their flocks on matters that can have a serious impact on their salvation. We also live in an age where there is a general lack of accountability. Our children see this behavior modeled in politicians and celebrities—it has become fashionable not to admit our bad choices. We no longer seem to look at how our personal decisions affect others. In the name of tolerance and in the fear of being judgmental, there's little sense of right or wrong. When these lines become blurred, so do the definitions of sin and the need to be absolved from it.

Many Catholics I talk with believe that Confession is reserved for grave or *mortal* sin. They honestly feel that this sacrament doesn't apply to them. I remember talking to one man from my own parish who told me he hadn't been to Confession in over fifteen years because he hadn't done anything that *bad*. It's understandable why this man thinks this way. With sin being a subject that is rarely preached about from the pulpit today (at least at the Masses I've attended), confusion exists over what constitutes a grave and mortal sin. Many don't understand, for example, that missing Mass on

Sunday without a serious reason, or using contraception, falls into the category of mortal sin. The lack of understanding of what sin is and why we need God's healing mercy in our lives makes the Sacrament of Reconciliation lose its importance in the eyes of the faithful.

Other Hurdles to Overcome

In addition to confusion over sin, there are other reasons that keep people away from the Sacrament of Reconciliation. Identifying these obstacles can help us to take steps to overcome them.

Let Go of Embarrassment

Admittedly, it's not easy or pleasant for most of us to talk about things we've done wrong. Feelings of embarrassment, anxiety, or shame can keep us away from receiving God's forgiveness—sometimes for years. Many fall into the trap of thinking that they are unforgivable, but as Jesus told Saint Faustina, *"the greater the sinner, the greater the right he has to My mercy"* (D 723).

Anticipating what the priest might think of us is another common obstacle that can keep people away from receiving God's gift of forgiveness. We may think that what we tell the priest will shock or surprise him. But the reality is, priests have heard it all before. I once had a priest tell me that by the second year of priesthood, there wasn't anything new anyone could tell him in the confessional. The good news is, because the priest has heard it all before, he is perfectly equipped to give us good counsel for our problems so we can overcome them. Sometimes people are concerned that the priest might tell others about what they hear in the confessional or that he might hold it against them. The fact is, priests are bound under severe penalties to keep absolute secrecy regarding sins that have been confessed to them. What is talked about in the confessional is sealed in the sacrament. I also like to think that God gives priests the grace to be able to let go of what they hear in the sacrament. Otherwise, it could be pretty overwhelming to hear thousands of confessions.

Move on from Bad Experiences

Sometimes an individual has had a bad experience in Confession and refuses to go back. Maybe he or she received poor advice from the priest one day or received a less-than-charitable response from him. It happens; priests are human. We can all probably recall a time when we received a report from a medical doctor or an insurance company that didn't sit well with us. Did we give up on doctors or insurance agents entirely? Or did we get a second opinion? But how many of us would think to consult a second priest in a spiritual matter, just to be sure we are hearing what God wants us to hear?

Understand the Need for the Priest

Even when they understand the reality of sin and the importance of being reconciled to God, many Catholics are unclear about the necessity of going to a priest to receive absolution. Why can't we confess our sins directly to God?

Jesus instituted the Sacrament of Reconciliation when he breathed on the Apostles and said to them, *"Receive the Holy Spirit. If you forgive the sins of any, they are forgiven; if you retain the sins of any, they are retained."* (John 20: 22–23 RSV) This ability to forgive sins was passed on to other disciples by the Apostles. God has ordained that his forgiveness is channeled through his chosen priests. He empowers them to forgive. God in his great wisdom knew it would be humbling to admit our faults in the presence of another human, but that it would be more effective that way. Since we are unable to see ourselves objectively, we need the guidance of someone on the outside who has our best spiritual interest in mind. I like to remind people in my talks that our confession is a gift to the priest as well. It does him good to see the love and mercy of God at work in people's lives. Wise priests, bishops, and popes use this sacrament frequently themselves.

Most Catholics have a basic understanding that sin hurts our individual relationships with God. A point that is less understood, however, is that sin ruptures our relationship with each another *and* with the Church. Because we have become members of the body of Christ through baptism, what we do (or what we fail to do) affects the entire community of believers as well as the spiritual well-being of the Church. In the early centuries of Christianity, this relationship was more obvious because sin was treated as a public affair. A sinner sat on the steps of the church in sackcloth and ashes for days, weeks, or even years, depending on the gravity of his sins. He was considered outside of the church community until his penance was served. As the practice to hear confessions privately became the norm, the effect of personal sin on the Church at large became less obvious. But the rupture remained there nonetheless. This is why, for the times we've gone astray, we need the priest in his collar as the sign and the instrument of God's merciful love for sinners, to represent the Church receiving us back into the fold. The Church, through the priest, forgives our sins in the name of Jesus Christ. In restoring ruptured relationships, the Sacrament of Reconciliation revitalizes the life of the Church.

Building a Positive Perception

How do we address—and heal—the plethora of negative attitudes and perceptions surrounding the Sacrament of Reconciliation? I believe the first step is education. I encourage Catholic adults, particularly those who are raising children in the faith or teaching them in a Catholic classroom, to take a new look at the sacrament from an adult perspective.

- Discover why Christ so prudently established this ongoing source of healing and strengthening for Christian living.
- Talk to a person you can trust—such as a priest, sister, or DRE who can help you work through any lingering questions or concerns you may have.
- Spend time in prayer with the Holy Spirit and ask him to show you where in your life you need healing and strengthening.
- Finally, receive the sacrament, regardless of how you feel about it. Let God work through it to touch your heart. Go regularly—monthly is a wonderful goal and a healthy balance. It is only through this ongoing exposure to God's mercy and forgiveness

that our attitudes will change and our hearts and minds will become ready to listen to our Creator and apply his will in our lives.

If we remain burdened with negative perceptions of the Sacrament of Reconciliation and aloof to its restorative power, we not only deny ourselves of God's great gift—we deny our children that right as well. Too many young Catholics receive the Sacrament of Reconciliation at the time they are preparing for First Holy Communion and then are not seen again until preparation for Confirmation. That's six or seven long and formative years that children miss out on the gift of forgiveness, healing, strengthening, and direction. What's more, the less frequently a child goes to Confession, the harder it is to make a good one, particularly as the sins become more serious.

What is required for people to truly appreciate the Sacrament of Reconciliation is a complete mindset change. We need to stop thinking of the sacrament as something reserved only for grave situations, and begin regarding it as an important source of grace to help us avoid sin and grow in holiness. This is wonderfully illustrated by Catholic author/ speaker/musician Vinny Flynn in an article that compares Confession to, of all things, car maintenance! In "A Spiritual Maintenance Agreement," Mr. Flynn points out that many car owners wait until their car breaks down before they take it in for service. He says many Catholics treat the Sacrament of Reconciliation with the same attitude. They wait until something is terribly broken in their lives before they go to Confession. Smart car owners, Mr. Flynn contends, take their cars in for an oil change and a check-up regularly, to avoid the chance of bigger problems down the road. Confession should be thought of in the same way. When we go to Confession regularly for the small things in our lives, they won't have the tendency to grow into bigger things later on. Our way of thinking about the sacrament changes from *repair* to *maintenance.*

Grace and Forgiveness: The Two-Part Gift of Reconciliation

Most Catholics are aware that in the Sacrament of Reconciliation, we receive something important: God's forgiveness for our sins. God's forgiveness is awesome. It's complete and unconditional. It doesn't come with strings attached like we might be tempted to do with our own forgiveness. God loves each of us no matter what we've done and is ready to forgive us, just for the asking. That means we can start all over again with a clean slate. Think of it like the ultimate do-over—that's a guarantee we just can't get anywhere else.

The person who taught me this lesson most poignantly was a priest named Fr. Patrick Martin, who preached a mission at my parish a number of years ago. Fr. Martin is a virtually blind priest who helped me and my fellow parishioners see God's love and mercy in a new and powerful way. His stories touched us deeply, and in our brokenness, we responded. During the three days he was with us, he spent over fourteen hours hearing confessions and counseling people. People's hearts were opened at Fr. Patrick's message of hope and healing, and they were eager to be restored to God's grace again through the Sacrament of Reconciliation.

But God's forgiveness, as wonderful as it is, is only one part of the gift that we receive in the Sacrament of Reconciliation. The second gift we receive is the gift of *grace,* and it is this grace that enables our hearts to be converted. This grace of the sacrament is manifested in a variety of ways. For example, when we go to Confession on a regular basis, we begin to see ourselves as God sees us. We gain the clarity to recognize habits and patterns in our lives that may be causing us to stumble. We learn to recognize attitudes behind our sins and to find out what's at the core of these attitudes. This is a key discovery we need to make in order to implement the necessary changes in our lives. Over time, Confession helps us to form our consciences in order for us to progress in holiness.

Going to Confession regularly helps us not only to recognize our weaknesses and temptations—it gives us strength *against* them so that we may triumph over character flaws and grow in virtue. Each time we come out of the confessional, we are fortified a little more against the one who sends us these temptations. One poignant testimony of the power of Confession is from Fr. Gabriel Amorth, the former official exorcist of Rome and the author of *An Exorcist Tells His Story*. Fr. Amorth, who has a great deal of expertise in the area of demonic infestation, oppression, obsession, and possession, repeatedly asserts that a good Confession is more powerful than any exorcism. Is it any wonder then that with the decline in the practice of Confession in the past several decades has come a sharp increase in various forms of evil?

Finally, going to Confession on a regular basis helps us become more loving and forgiving, not only to ourselves, but to those around us. We become less judgmental and critical as we experience God's love and forgiveness working in our lives. These are all-important, life-changing graces. That's why it is so valuable to receive the sacrament on a regular basis to help us deal with all that life brings our way.

Forgiveness Starts at Home

I can't think of a better place to live out the concept of reconciliation than in our own homes. As we all know, when a group of people resides under the same roof, it's only a matter of time before someone sins against another. It's just our human nature. As parents, we have the opportunity to raise our children with the mindset that all of us (ourselves first and foremost) need to be accountable to others for offenses we've committed against them. When we practice asking for and receiving forgiveness from one another at home, it builds our relationships with those in our family and makes us feel better about ourselves. For children raised with this mentality, going to Confession is a natural progression. The same techniques can be applied in the classroom to effectively teach children accountability and compassion.

Preparation Activities

For those families preparing a child for the first time for the Sacrament of Reconciliation, there are a number of suggestions I can offer to help make this time meaningful and positive.

Celebrate as a Family

First, celebrate the sacrament regularly and as a family. Young children who have the experience of watching their parents and older siblings make a Confession will eagerly await the day that they, too, will be able to participate in this special ritual. Most parishes today offer a Communal Penance celebration, usually during Lent or Advent. The celebration typically opens with a few prayers and songs before people are invited to make a private confession with one of the numerous priests set up at different stations throughout the church. A child making the sacrament for the first time is encouraged by seeing lots of family members, classmates, neighbors, and teachers happy to receive God's forgiveness.

Act Out a Confession at Home

One of the activities you can try with a youngster who may have anxious feelings about the sacrament is to act out a confession at home. Let the child play both the priest and the penitent, so he can get comfortable with the role of each. Another technique my husband and I have found helpful on occasion is to share our own experiences of Confession with our children. Granted, not everything parents discuss in the confessional is going to be appropriate for little ears, but there are opportunities for us to talk about struggles we are having in our own lives and why we turn to Confession for help. For example, one of the most common reasons I find myself in the confessional is my lack of patience and the way I can yell at my children. My children are aware of this character flaw of mine, because they are the recipients of my anger! But when my boys know that mommy struggles with her lack of patience and goes to Father so-in-so in Confession to ask for God's help, it inspires them to use the sacrament for the things that they find troubling in their own lives.

Write a Letter to Jesus

Another idea came to me when our second child was preparing to make his first Confession. About a week before, I suggested to Nicholas that he go to his bedroom, say a little prayer, and write a letter to Jesus about how he felt going to Confession and what was on his heart that he might like to talk about with the priest. After a while, Nicholas returned from his bedroom with a letter in his hand. I hadn't asked to see the letter, but he wanted to share it with us, anyway. It was precious, written straight from a child's heart. The following week, when the day to make his first Confession arrived, Nicholas was not at all nervous. He didn't feel anxious about what he was going to say or worried that he might forget something. He simply folded his letter and put it in the back pocket of his pants and took it with him to church. When it was his turn to meet with the priest, he took out his letter and read it aloud. The priest praised Nicholas afterward for a good Confession and suggested he do it again the next time. It really made the experience positive for everyone, particularly Nicholas, and it has prompted me on occasion to jot down some thoughts during the week when I'm preparing for my own Confessions. If you try this activity of writing a letter to Jesus in the classroom, do not collect, read, or grade the letters. This is a personal experience meant for the child, the confessor, and God.

Preparing for a Visitor

A few decades ago, there was some experimentation in this country regarding the Sacrament of Reconciliation. Some Catholic educators seemed influenced by psychologists at the time who rejected the idea that children were capable of committing or understanding sin until a much older age than seven. Some dioceses (including mine at one point) permitted parents to delay taking their children to Confession for the first time until they felt they were ready—anytime up until fourth grade. I strongly disagree with the notion that children are incapable of understanding the concept of sin at a young age. It was always remarkable to me with each one of our four boys just how quickly they would understand when they had deliberately done something wrong. Their pride and embarrassment may have prevented them from readily admitting it at first, just as it can with us adults, but they knew just the same. Children are capable of a great deal more than we tend to give them credit for.

The children I have had the pleasure to speak with in Catholic classrooms are for the most part eager to make the Sacrament of Reconciliation, because they see it as a rite of passage. It makes them feel grown-up. At the same time, they are understandably nervous. One of the points I like to make with children in second grade is that there is no better way to prepare for their First Holy Communion than to make their First Reconciliation. To illustrate, I take them through the following exercise. I ask them to imagine that a very special visitor was coming to their house—someone really important. Perhaps a king or a president or their favorite professional athlete. We talk about the kinds of things their family might do to prepare for the visit. Perhaps they would clean the house, make special food, or put on nice clothes. I then tell them that very soon Jesus Christ, the most special guest of all, is coming to their house—their *heart*. We want to make sure it is all clean and ready to receive this very special guest, and the best way to do that is through the Sacrament of Reconciliation.

Confession for the Past, Encouragement for the Future

Going to Confession regularly with a priest who knows us and is willing to challenge us on our journey in faith can have similar benefits to spiritual direction, although it's important to clarify that Confession is not intended to be spiritual direction or personal counseling. We're not supposed to walk into a confessional on a Saturday afternoon and chew the pastor's ear about our feelings and emotions for an hour, seeking his advice to help us to work out our problems. First of all, that's not considerate to the people standing in line behind us. Second, this is not the purpose of the sacrament. Our responsibility is to carefully examine our consciences prior to making a Confession and to be prepared to walk in and name our sins without excuses or sugar-coating. The priest will often provide some brief advice in this exchange to help us in the practice of virtue and for our ongoing conversion and growth in the spiritual life. Through our careful self-reflection and honest sharing with the priest, and our willingness to correct the course in our lives in the areas he points out, we reap therapeutic and spiritual benefits from the Sacrament of Reconciliation. It truly helps shape us into good followers of Christ. For extensive help in dealing with emotional, psychological, or social issues, however, we do best to arrange a meeting with a priest at a separate time to determine whether this is something he can provide counsel for, or if we need to seek professional assistance.

I once heard a priest talk about Confession as being not just about the sins we've committed in the past, as important as this is, but about the sins we are going to come up against in the future. As fallible human beings, we all continue to sin. There's no way of getting around it. But it is most consoling to know there is a tool and source of grace out there—the Sacrament of Reconciliation—that can minimize the number of times and degree in which we wander off the path. For all of these reasons, Reconciliation is a gift and a celebration. That's how God intended it to be. If we can help people see that Reconciliation is a way to be close to the heart of Jesus, to hear him whispering encouragement in our ears, and to feel the warmth of his arms around us as we are forgiven and sent out anew, I truly believe people will return to this sacrament with enthusiasm—and your own family will learn to embrace it with joy.

Looking Ahead...

Our merciful God knew we would be inclined to sin after baptism. His antidote: the Sacrament of Reconciliation! We've learned how sin ruptures our relationship with Christ and his Church. We've seen how greatly misunderstood and underutilized this powerful sacrament is, with its gift of forgiveness and grace. Now we're ready to harness the power and promise of this sacrament. We've learned ways to prepare for and celebrate this sacrament as a family, not just for major repairs, but also for "spiritual maintenance." Nourished by the Sacrament of Reconciliation, our hearts are ready to receive the subject of the next chapter, the Sacrament of Holy Communion.

3

SACRAMENT OF SACRAMENTS

Holy Communion

The Sacrament of Eucharist or Holy Communion is the center and summit of Catholic life. Our understanding of how, by the power of the Holy Spirit through the office of the priest, ordinary bread and wine are transformed into the body, blood, soul, and divinity of Jesus Christ sets us apart from other Christian faiths. While we've seen that Christ is present in all of the sacraments, he is present in Holy Communion in a special and powerful way—a *substantial* way—that eclipses the others. In this sacrament, we are united to Christ, who makes us sharers in his body and blood to form a single body, the Church. The Eucharist is the means God has selected to remain with us until the end of time, and for that hearts are filled with *praise and thanksgiving*, which is what the word *Eucharist* means in Greek. How unspeakably marvelous it is for the King and Creator of the universe to humble himself under the ordinary appearances of bread and wine just so he can dwell among his people in such an intimate fashion!

The Real Deal

The concept of Jesus—the same Jesus who walked the earth 2,000 years ago—being truly present in this sacrament has always been mind-boggling to me. To realize that Our Lord dwells in every tabernacle in every Catholic parish around the world, just waiting for us to visit him, is absolutely incredible. For some converts to the Catholic faith, as well as for some Catholics who have fallen away from the faith, the belief in the Real Presence in the Eucharist can be a stumbling block. This was not the case with me. As with other sacraments, God graciously assisted me with understanding the Eucharist. The first Mass I ever attended was on my college campus with the man who would eventually become my husband. It was a rather small and casual gathering compared to some of the Lutheran services I had attended. But in that Sunday night service, my eyes were opened. The moment the priest held up that consecrated host, I recognized Jesus, truly present. I did not need to be convinced theologically—I just *knew*. It was not a Damascus experience, like when Paul was thrown to the ground with thunderbolts and lightning. It was more like an Emmaus experience, the Scripture story of the two men conversing with a stranger on the road to Emmaus; they did not realize it was Jesus they were speaking to until he came to dine with them. At the breaking of the bread, their eyes were opened. My eyes were opened that day, too. I even remember thinking to myself, "Oh, so *that's* where you've been hiding!" It was the first time I truly experienced God in a public worship service, and it was a life-changing event. My love for the Eucharist has grown steadily stronger since. It is my hope and desire to help open the eyes of other

Catholics – adults and children alike – to the great miracle that is before them every time they attend Mass.

One of the greatest tragedies to me is to see Catholics growing indifferent toward this sacrament and even leaving Jesus Christ in the Eucharist because they have found a more energetic Christian congregation down the street. So that I could better understand what would cause such a decision, I've asked some fallen-away Catholics about their decision. Without exception, they tell me the same thing—they don't remember the Real Presence being heavily emphasized in their religious education. In their minds, church is church, and it's really all the same thing to God whether you worship in a Catholic church or any other Christian church. They focus on trying to live good lives. Other former Catholics who no longer practice any faith at all tell me they can remember hearing about things like the Real Presence, but they just never believed in "all that stuff." Somehow, the miracle of the Eucharist never became very miraculous for these individuals.

Pope Benedict XVI has called for a return to the basics in catechesis, and that's where we need to start when we educate our children (and ourselves) about the Sacrament of the Eucharist. The first step is to pray to fully embrace and convey very clearly that Jesus is truly present—body, blood, soul, and divinity—in the Sacrament of Holy Communion. For us, it's not a symbolic act—it's the real deal. Sometimes parents worry about how they can explain such a mystery to their children when they struggle to understand it themselves. Don't worry. As Thomas à Kempis said in *The Imitation of Christ,* it's not our job to solve God's mysteries. We are just asked to partake in them. No one will ever fully understand the mystical transformation that happens at the moment of consecration. But I've found that children are actually more open to accepting these things when we explain them in terms they can understand. They seem more capable of belief than we adults. We need to let them know that this is a uniquely Catholic (and Orthodox) belief, and that it is an important difference between our faith and others. Through the act of consecration, the bread and wine retain their physical appearances, but only to house the great miracle that has just happened—a complete transformation into the body and blood of Christ. It's not a partial or temporary change, for example as some Protestants claim, but a total and permanent change. This is true food that will give us eternal life.

Why do we believe such a remarkable claim? Because Jesus said it:

> *I am the living bread which came down from heaven; if any one eats of this bread, he will live forever, and the bread which I shall give for the life of the world is my flesh... Truly, truly, I say to you, unless you eat the flesh of the Son of man and drink his blood, you have no life in you; he who eats my flesh and drinks my blood has eternal life, and I will raise him up at the last day. For my flesh is food indeed and my blood is drink indeed. He who eats my flesh and drinks my blood abides in me, and I in him.*
>
> *(John 6:51–54, RSV)*

These words are powerful and hard to interpret in any other way than how Jesus meant them: that is, literally. Those who were present to hear these words from Jesus' mouth that day certainly understood him to be speaking literally. They clearly heard what he was saying and were aghast. *How could this man give us his flesh and blood to eat?* they puzzled among themselves. Many walked away from Jesus that day because of this "hard teaching." We are given the same choice today. Are we going to walk away from this miracle, too, and potentially relinquish the promise of eternal life? Or is our belief strong enough to accept what we can only perceive with the eyes of faith?

Preparing for and Responding to the Eucharist

The Sacrament of Holy Communion is a foretaste of the wedding feast of the Lamb, the heavenly banquet that awaits us in the New Jerusalem. When we eat this bread and drink this cup, we proclaim the death of the Lord until he comes again in glory. In doing this, we also proclaim the forgiveness of sins. Through our intimate union with Christ, the sacrament of the Eucharist cleanses us from past venial sins and protects us from future sins. This is not to say that it makes us *immune* to sin; rather, it makes us spiritually stronger to avoid sin in the future.

Questions for Examining Our Conscience

Once we understand the reality of the Eucharist, we should be inspired us to treat this sacrament with the utmost respect and love, beginning with a genuflection or deep bow in the direction of the tabernacle when we enter the sanctuary. It also commands of us careful preparation for Holy Communion through a thoughtful examination of conscience and being judicious so that we are in a state of grace when we receive the Lord. For example, my husband and I take our children through a list of general questions to reflect on their actions during the past week. We may ask them to consider the following:

- Have I been selfish or greedy?
- Have I spoken badly about others?
- Have I been forgetting my prayers?
- Did I lose my temper?
- Did I take something that didn't belong to me?
- Have I been wide-awake and attentive for TV but distracted and restless in church?

Questions like these help all of us recognize the areas we need to work on and redirect our actions and attitudes to become better followers of Jesus.

Before the Eucharist

It is fitting to spend time contemplating what we are about to receive in the Sacrament of Holy Communion, for it is a great gift that we are being given. The Eucharist is the food for the journey of conversion. It nourishes our faith and makes us more Christ-like. It heals us and refreshes us. It gives us the fortitude to be more resistant to our temptations. As I tell young people, the Eucharist is like a super vitamin pill for the soul. I remind them that we should receive this gift with deep respect, awe, and humility. I ask them to think about how the people of the Old Testament revered the word of God carved on stone tablets. The word was so sacred it was contained in a special ark that no one could touch without permission. Now we have the word of God *made flesh*—Jesus Christ—and that is worthy of far more honor. The Virgin Mary (sometimes referred to as the "new ark") received Jesus into her body with great love, respect, praise, honor, joy, and thanksgiving. We are called to do the same as we prepare to take this same Jesus into our bodies. This is a perfect time to ask God to use our life as he wishes, to be our true leader, and to help us be obedient followers. It is also an appropriate time to remember the needs of family and friends, both living and dead.

After the Eucharist

Once the sacrament is received, as I explain to children in my presentations, it is best to return to our seats and remain quiet to relish the presence of Jesus within us. This is not the time to talk or read the bulletin. I suggest they close their eyes and ponder how blessed we are that God would choose to be with us in such an intimate and beautiful way. Through this sacrament, we are filled with a powerful grace that can help us change our lives and grow in holiness. With the power of Jesus within us, we can become living instruments of his love, mercy, and peace to truly make a difference in this world. I tell my young audiences that the best prayer after Holy Communion is not words but action: to go in peace to love and serve the Lord. In other words, to live in love and do God's will. The Eucharist empowers us to do that.

The more we receive Jesus in the Eucharist, the more we will desire to receive him—not just on Sundays, but during the week when possible and on vacations as well.

We get to the point where we realize we just can't live without it, because it is Jesus who is abiding in us, just like he promises in Holy Scripture. Holy Communion is the consummation of our relationship with Christ. It is the most intimate way we can encounter Our Lord and Savior in this earthly life, until the day we are with him in heaven. If you are not experiencing this sense of falling deeper and deeper in love with Jesus Christ in the Eucharist, I suggest you try receiving more often with a prepared heart. Ask Jesus every time to open your eyes and mind and heart to this great gift and mystery. Allow him to work in you and through you. The transformation may be subtle at first. Others may recognize it in you before you do, but trust me when I say that transformation *will* happen. That's the beauty of all the sacraments.

Preparation Activities

Preparing a child for his or her First Holy Communion is an exciting time. There are gifts to buy, a dress or suit to pick out, a party to arrange, and friends and family to invite. But preparation for this sacrament is most effective when it begins long before the special day. Make use of the year prior to First Holy Communion to mark this milestone spiritual occasion, both for the communicant and your entire family.

When your son or daughter makes his or her First Holy Communion, he or she is joining the parish community in a holy meal that makes us one body. It makes us *family*. Jesus recognized the sacredness and bonding effect of the family meal, which is why he chose it as a way to be present to his people for all time. As a church family united in the holy meal of the Eucharist, we begin to recognize Christ in one another, particularly in the poor, the sick, the imprisoned, and the needy. We become Eucharistic people called to bring Jesus to others.

Start with the Family Meal

At home, the family dinner mirrors the meal that bonds us at church. Family meals are a sacred time, more precious than ever today with the demands of our busy lifestyles. Despite having kid activities on most nights of the week, my husband and I are fiercely protective of our mealtime and will look for creative ways to ensure we eat together as often as possible. Many families, including the one I grew up in, do not eat meals together, and they often lack intimacy as adults. I see the enormous benefit of the family meal with my own children. This is a time to pray, to reflect on our day, to share our highs and lows with one another, and to stay connected. It is a powerful ritual that goes far beyond its nutritional importance.

Pray and Read the Bible

The year your child is preparing for First Holy Communion is a time to pray often as a family for that child. Perhaps there is a sign or small banner that can be displayed in the home to remind everyone of the ongoing spiritual preparation that is happening to a member of the family. As our family has experienced, preparation for a new sacrament strengthens not only the individual receiving it, but the entire family. Parents and older siblings can use this time to share stories and memories about their own First Holy Communion. It's also a great time to read and reflect on Bible stories that prefigure this sacrament, such as the miracle of the loaves and fishes. In this story, Jesus prays over the meager supply of food and it miraculously becomes enough to feed the multitudes, with plenty to spare. The important part of this story is that Jesus commands *the Apostles*, his first priests, to feed the people with this miraculous food. He does not do it himself. He uses his priests today to perform the same function with the Eucharist. There is also the story of the wedding at Cana, Jesus' first public miracle. When the wine runs out at a wedding, Mary pleads with her Son to do something about it. Jesus alludes to the fact that his hour has not come (a reference to his impending sacrificial death), but still he instructs the servants to set several jars of water before him, which he turns into choice wine. This is proof that Jesus can transform one substance into another and is a foreshadowing of his blood, the new wine, that will be poured out for his people.

Share Your Experience

When our second son, Nicholas, was preparing for his First Holy Communion, I perceived an extraordinary spiritual readiness in him. It inspired me to write him a letter, sharing my own experiences with Holy Communion. In my letter I wrote about how all the angels and saints are gathered at the moment of consecration, and that heaven and earth are united in this special moment. I shared that receiving Jesus in my body was even more intimate of an experience than when I carried my children in my womb. The sacrament creates a longing in my heart for Jesus. After I gave the letter to Nicholas, it occurred to me that other parents might benefit from this shared personal reflection. I asked my son for permission to print the letter in our parish newsletter, and it turned out to have a positive effect on a number of parents who were subsequently inspired to write something similar for their own children.

Attend Holy Thursday Mass

Another preparation activity for First Holy Communion is to attend Holy Thursday Mass as a family. Holy Thursday is one of the most beautiful liturgical celebrations of the year as we commemorate the night Jesus gave us this holy meal. Priests and deacons perform the washing of the feet of twelve parishioners, imitating Jesus as he demonstrated this ultimate act of servitude for his Apostles. When I speak with Catholic schoolteachers, I encourage them to invite their students to celebrate this special event with their families. While you can't *require* a family to attend, you can offer extra credit or some incentive to inspire a few students to experience Holy Thursday Mass and share their reflections with the rest of the class after Easter break. If you've never attended this sacred liturgy, consider this your personal invitation.

Keep the Fire Burning!

Children who prepare for the Sacrament of Holy Communion for the first time usually have the anticipation and excitement worthy of such a great gift. But eventually, after receiving for a while, this excitement can wear off. It can become easy to forget what we are receiving in the sacrament and even become boring. As parents, we must work diligently to prevent our family's faith from growing lukewarm about the Eucharist. Ideally, we would like every reception to be like our First Holy Communion, and it can with proper prayer and preparation.

Reverence for the Blessed Sacrament

One of the last great acts of Pope John Paul II during his pontificate was to institute the Year of the Eucharist that took place from October 2004 to October 2005. The late pope recognized the importance of the Eucharist to the Catholic faith, and the need for the faithful to embrace this sacrament more fully. His intention in instituting a year focused on the Blessed Sacrament was to renew our fervor in the celebration and adoration of the Eucharist, and make it the center of our lives. Pope Benedict XVI, his successor, has continued to call the attention of the faithful to this sacrament and its powerful potential for transforming our lives, calling the Eucharist "the great school of love."

Eucharistic Adoration

Eucharistic Adoration, the practice of prayerfully acknowledging the Real Presence of Jesus in the consecrated elements, has roots that can be traced all the way back to the early Church community. It could be said that the first holy hour of prayer was actually made by the Apostles in the garden of Gethsemane, shortly before the arrest of Jesus.

But certainly, the understanding of Jesus' presence in the consecrated bread and wine commanded reverence among the faithful at the dawn of the Church. Over the centuries, customs began that incorporated an extended period of time of adoration before the Blessed Sacrament, such as the devotion of 40 hours, and eventually, even perpetual adoration. While Eucharistic Adoration typically refers to the Blessed Sacrament exposed in a monstrance on an altar, it can also refer to adoration before the closed tabernacle as well.

A Renewed Practice

The Second Vatican Council in the 1960s called for a renewal in the practice of Eucharistic Adoration, and Pope John Paul II, an active participant in that Council, was the first to institute Eucharistic Adoration in St. Peter's Basilica (1981). Since then, there has been a strong resurgence of Eucharistic Adoration in parishes and religious houses around the world. Pope Benedict XVI echoes the importance of a renewed practice of Eucharistic Adoration globally. He, like his predecessor, recognizes the Eucharist as our source of hope, and the best way to establish everlasting peace on earth. His desire is for every parish to take on this reverent devotion.

Parishes that have instituted a program of Eucharistic Adoration, particularly perpetual adoration in which there are one to two adorers at all times before the Blessed Sacrament, have reaped tremendous spiritual rewards. Entire books are written about the remarkable experiences that happen when a parish helps to cultivate in its parishioners a sense of awe before Jesus' presence in the Eucharist. There are countless examples of renewed faith, conversions of heart, physical miracles, restored relationships, and an increase of vocations to the religious life that have happened when this prayerful practice is employed.

Adoration in the Classroom

When I met with the teaching staff at a Catholic school in California a few years ago, the question came up about how to help students become enthusiastic about their faith when there was no support for this at home. Many families, they told me, had situations going on at home that were in direct conflict with Catholic morals and teaching, sending a confused message to students. This is a problem that is common in many parochial schools today, and one that will not be solved by humans alone. My advice to the teachers was to let God resolve this one. How? By taking their students before the Blessed Sacrament for ten minutes every Friday during the school year. I told the teachers not to have the students pray aloud or read or sing, but to simply kneel in silence before the tabernacle for the whole ten minutes. For some children, at least at first, this might seem like an eternity, but I assured the teachers the students would get used to it. Once the initial giggling and distractions wore off, the children would begin to settle down and listen. And they would begin to *hear*. God has the power to ignite souls, and schools that attempt this with their students will see a transformation, not just in the students, but in the teachers and the families as well.

Jesus Is Worth It

My own experience of Eucharistic Adoration has been tremendously positive. While our parish does not have a program implemented, a neighboring parish does, and my husband and I initially signed on as substitute adorers. Sometimes we would get a call to cover a daytime hour, and I would bring with me whatever small child I had at home at the time knowing that we would be the only adorers there. During our hour, we would talk about Jesus being present in the tabernacle, and how we should act in his presence. We would kneel before him and perhaps read a Bible story, or pray the Rosary. We would pray aloud for the people in our lives, and sometimes the little ones would color a picture about Jesus. Considering their young age, it was not realistic to expect them to sit in silence for an hour. I had to keep their focus on why we were there. Eventually, my husband and I became regular adorers, and we have signed up for an 11:00 p.m. hour on Sunday nights. Sometimes we go alone for the hour, depending on the next day's schedule, but more often we make the hour together. We use the twenty-minute drive to pray aloud, thanking God for all his blessings in our lives and for giving us the opportunity to adore him in this special way. We also use that time to list all the people and situations for which we are dedicating our hour. Once we arrive at the chapel, we are ready to *listen*. Often, we'll spend the first half hour on our knees or even lying prostrate before the tabernacle, quieting our minds from distractions and constantly refocusing on Jesus. The second half of the hour might be spent in reading Scripture or discussing what we've been hearing in our hearts.

Our time before the Blessed Sacrament gives my husband and me strength and peace. It often helps give us clarity on a situation with which we are wrestling. Sometimes I take a manuscript or a project the two of us might be working on for a blessing from Jesus, and for insight on what else might need to be done with it. There have been times when we don't hear an answer to a question we might have, and that can be frustrating. But we try to remember what a priest friend told us about adoration. He said it is a time to bask in the Son, to get "radiated" by his love and mercy. Our hearts may be being prepared while we don't even know it. Sometimes I just sense comfort in going before the Blessed Sacrament. Other times fatigue may overtake me and I may find myself dozing. A few precious times, the power I've felt emanating from that tabernacle has been so strong it's all I can do to remain on my knees. But it is in seeing the positive growth overall that brings my husband and me back to the Blessed Sacrament each week, even if it means getting out of a warm bed and driving out into the cold, rain or snow. Jesus is worth it.

Eucharistic Miracles

One of the first subjects I began studying as a new Catholic was supernatural wonders—particularly, Eucharistic miracles. By this I mean times in history when God saw fit to make a *physical* change occur in the consecrated host or wine. These miracles would often occur during times in history when people (even, at times, the priests themselves) had doubts about the Real Presence. Consecrated hosts might suddenly become encircled with flesh, or drip blood, right on the altar in front of the entire congregation. Consecrated wine might coagulate into pellets of blood in the chalice. The Eucharist has also been known at times to survive floods and fire and even thievery. These extraordinary and supernatural events have been, and continue to be, signs that the Blessed Sacrament is not something to be taken lightly. Most young people and their parents are unaware of wonders like Eucharistic miracles. It seems that some of these supernatural occurrences in our faith have been downplayed in recent decades. But they are not to be forgotten, as they can greatly encourage the faithful. Looking back at my own faith journey, I remember reading these stories as a new Catholic and being awe-inspired and uplifted all the more in God's power and presence through this sacrament.

In my speaking on the topic, I've found a ready audience of young and not-so-young Catholics who are equally inspired by these stories.[3] It is my hope to engage Catholic teenagers and young adults in particular with the reality of God's love for us through amazing feats like the stigmata, incorrupt bodies, apparitions, unusual abilities of the saints, weeping statues and artwork, and of course, miracles of the Eucharist. With the rising interest in the supernatural today, as demonstrated by the plethora of movies, television programs, and books that center on fantasy, science fiction, super-human powers, magic, and the like, I think young Catholics will find the supernatural miracles of our Catholic faith equally engaging. The important difference, of course, is that these miracles are not computer-generated. They are *real*.

The Miracle of the Mass

As a final reflection on the Sacrament of Holy Communion, let us consider the Mass, which is the typical way most of us receive the Eucharist. Judging by the decrease in Mass attendance today, it would seem that something has gone terribly wrong with people's understanding of this great gift. Many people don't attend Mass at all, or they attend only out of habit or obligation. But how many of us go out of genuine love? If people understood better what the Mass really was— nothing short of a miracle–they would come with ready hearts. Mass is an ancient and sacred ritual that has been carefully preserved and passed down through the centuries. It is celebrated much the same way throughout the world, with the same readings and responses. The only variation is the language and, in some cases, cultural customs, such as African dance or Mariachi music. I've had the pleasure of experiencing a universal Mass in Lourdes, the well-known shrine of Our Lady in France, where I participated in worship with thousands of people from around the world. The Gospel there is preached in four languages, and the liturgy is punctuated with Latin responses, which we could all pray together. This experience really helped me to appreciate the universality of our faith.

Mass is the most perfect way to praise God. It's an excellent place to hear God speak to us through word and song. It's also great for helping us to discern our special purpose in life (we'll be talking about that in the next chapter on Confirmation) and for gaining strength against our temptations. I've found that the more we participate in Mass, the more we get out of it. This doesn't just mean actively singing and praying, although that's important, but also participating as altar servers, Extraordinary Ministers, ushers, and gift bearers, or lending our talents in the music ministry. But the true miracle of Mass, and the center of it all, is what takes place at consecration. In this moment, as I like to tell young people, it's like we're mystically transported in a time machine back to Jerusalem 2,000 years ago, to the foot of the cross at Calvary, where we can witness the ultimate sacrifice of Jesus who died once and for all of us. This event was so significant that God wants all of us to be a part of it, not just the small crowd of people who were gathered on Calvary that fateful day and witnessed it directly. At every Mass, we experience that history-changing moment, if we open our hearts and minds to the miracle.

The Church considers Mass an obligation because we are obligated as Christians to never lose sight of the great act of sacrificial love that has freed us from death and has made eternal life with God possible. Going to Mass at least once a week helps us to keep that thought fresh in our minds. Just as importantly, the graces that are available to us at Mass are essential for our spiritual survival. The Church, like any good parent, knows what is best for us and gives us structure and guidelines. She tells us to attend Mass much like we tell our children to brush their teeth and eat their vegetables. They may not see the long-term benefits, but we do. In the same manner, so does the Church. Once we begin asking God to help us appreciate the great gift of the Mass, we will cringe when we hear it being referred to as an "obligation." Because for us it will not be something we *have* to do but something we *want* to do: a joy, a miracle, and a necessity in our lives.

Looking Ahead...

All of the sacraments enable us to encounter God. Yet, as we've learned, the Sacrament of Holy Communion (or Eucharist) is unique, because of the Real Presence of Jesus Christ, Body, Blood, Soul, and Divinity. Such a sacrament deserves attentiveness before, during, and after our reception of it. So sacred is the Eucharist, it has become the focus of adoration and miracles. In this chapter, we've looked at ways our families can develop a greater appreciation and understanding of this central part of our Catholic faith. We begin to recognize how the Eucharist spiritually equips us to do the works of God, which is a primary task I'll be discussing in our next chapter on the Sacrament of Confirmation.

4

SEALED WITH THE SPIRIT

The Sacrament of Confirmation

Confirmation is considered to be the completion of baptism because it deepens and intensifies the gifts of the Spirit that we received at our first sacrament. In the Sacrament of Confirmation we affirm the promises that were made on our behalf at our baptism and declare our own intention to follow Christ. Through it, we are more perfectly bound to the Church and enriched with a special strength of the Holy Spirit. In Confirmation, each of us receives the charge to be true witnesses of Christ, called to spread and defend the faith by word and deed.

The Origin of the Sacrament

The Jews of the Old Testament believed that the Spirit of the Lord would rest upon the long-awaited Messiah. This would be the sign that he was with God. At Jesus' baptism in the Jordan River by John the Baptist, the Holy Spirit did indeed descend, fulfilling the ancient prophecy. During his mission, Jesus promised his Apostles that there would be a further outpouring of the Spirit. This was fulfilled at Pentecost, when the Apostles were ignited by the Holy Spirit and sent forth to proclaim the Good News. Despite speaking in different languages, they were understood by the multitudes, and they performed great works in the name of Jesus. The Apostles in turn baptized the believers and, laying hands upon them, imparted the gift of the Holy Spirit. Perfumed oil called chrism was soon included in the ritual to symbolize cleansing and strengthening, as well as healing, comfort, and health; it also served as a sign of consecration.

In the early Church, the Sacrament of Confirmation immediately followed baptism and was always conferred by the bishop to emphasize the connection to the Apostles and to Jesus. As the Church grew in number, it became unwieldy for one bishop to visit all the newly baptized. Therefore, the rite of Confirmation was moved to a later time in life, which is generally how it is conferred today. (The exception is when adults are baptized, in which case Confirmation follows immediately after.)

Protestant versus Catholic Confirmation

I consider myself doubly blessed to have had two Confirmation experiences. The first took place in my Lutheran church when I was fifteen years old. Although nine years of Sunday school and Sunday worship had not made a tremendous impact on me, the day of my Confirmation left a vivid impression. I wore a white gown over my new dress, and a party was scheduled afterward. The white gown seemed to symbolize that my classmates and I were graduating—moving on. For most of us, it meant moving *out*. I was no exception—it wasn't long after my Confirmation that my church attendance began to drop. As other life interests became more important, worshipping God was moved to a back burner.

What I find interesting about my Lutheran Confirmation is the disparity between what I thought Confirmation meant back then and what my church actually taught. Somehow, I had gotten it into my head that the Holy Spirit would descend upon me at the moment I was confirmed. In my design for the cover of our Confirmation program, I included three doves, symbolizing the unmistakable presence of the Holy Spirit. I remember standing at the altar surrounded by my parents, my aunt and uncle (my baptismal godparents), and the pastor, who were all laying hands on me in prayer. I felt a strong sense of power in that moment and mistakenly interpreted that as the Holy Spirit. But as I would find out much later, the Lutheran Church does not consider Confirmation a sacrament. It's looked at as a rite, in which the confirmand (the person being confirmed) makes a public confession of faith. There is no Holy Spirit summoned and no grace conferred, despite my vivid imagination. I can only attribute the power I felt that day to the fact that this was my first experience of being prayed over, which in itself is a powerful experience regardless of one's faith.

Perhaps my Lutheran Confirmation was a foreshadowing of my second Confirmation, as I entered the Catholic Church in 1983. The event took place in the Lady Chapel behind the main altar of St. Patrick's Cathedral in New York, with my fiancé serving as my sponsor. I had been living and working in Manhattan at the time and taking my RCIA instruction there, so it was the appointed location for the liturgical celebration. I'm certain I did not fully appreciate the significance of the Mass being held in the cathedral of one of the largest cities in the world. I barely noticed the looming statue of the Virgin Mary behind us (visible in the pictures taken that day), although the Blessed Mother would become an active part of my spirituality.

There were no unusual experiences that day as my head was anointed with chrism oil and I received the Eucharist for the first time. I was not asked to give a Confirmation name and there was no face slapping. There wasn't even a bishop in attendance (not that I would have known the difference at the time); the priest who taught our RCIA class presided over the liturgy. It was a small, simple ceremony. The Holy Spirit had indeed descended in my Catholic Sacrament of Confirmation, but just like in the story of Elijah in the cave, God did not manifest himself that day in an earthquake or a fire, but in a small, still voice. And with that came a sense of peace and satisfaction that I had done the right thing. It was a quiet commitment and the beginning of my journey as a Catholic.

A Serious Commitment

In reality, I was no more knowledgeable about the meaning of my Catholic Confirmation than I had been of my Lutheran one (although I did get it right about the presence of the Holy Spirit.) I had no idea back then that I was receiving special strength to be able to witness and evangelize to others about the Catholic faith, which is precisely what this sacrament requires of us, and I *certainly* had no idea of the public way God would eventually use me to do just that. At the time I only saw this as a private rite of passage for myself. This seems to be the same mindset of many young Catholics today as they prepare for the Sacrament of Confirmation. It is looked upon as a graduation, a rite of passage, and for many, sadly, an excuse for not having to go to church or any type of religious education any more.

I remember sitting in on a meeting between the DRE of my parish and a new class of confirmands. The DRE, aware that there were a number of unfamiliar faces in the audience, pointed in the direction of the baptismal font. She told the young people that fourteen years ago, their parents had carried them to that font, or one like it, to have them baptized. Their parents had made a commitment back then to raise their child in the faith, to take him or her to Mass on Sunday and see that he or she was prepared properly for the sacraments. "If your parents haven't been taking you to Mass every Sunday," she continued, knowing full well that they hadn't, "they have been breaking their promise to you." This comment was received with a number of raised eyebrows and even a few scowls. I'm sure the teenagers were considering the irony of the situation: their parents expected them to keep their commitments and promises, but why weren't Mom and Dad doing the same? I'll bet there were some interesting conversations in a few homes that evening.

This is the first point I wish to make about the Sacrament of Confirmation. As stated in the chapter on baptism, it's truly important for parents to understand the commitment we are making when we bring our children before the Lord to receive his sacraments. It's not fair to our children to prepare them for First Reconciliation and First Holy Communion like it is a super big deal, let them flounder for the next six years while sports and other interests force the practice of our faith to the back burner, and then, when

Confirmation time comes, suddenly resurrect the faith again. Children should not be on spiritual vacation during these important growing years, and neither should we. These are vital years in a child's life that deserve to be nourished by a continued growth in faith through religious classes at school or afterschool catechesis, frequent use of the sacraments, and supplemental efforts at home.

Once young people reach the age of Confirmation, they must be carefully prepared for what they are about to undertake. Confirmation preparation should be oriented toward developing an intimate relationship with Jesus Christ and a growing affinity for the Holy Spirit. If, after being presented with the proper catechism for the sacrament, some of the young people decide they are not ready or able to make this sacrament, they should not be forced to do so. The sacrament has to be received with an open heart and a free will, just like the Sacrament of Matrimony or Holy Orders. This is a serious commitment we are making to the Lord and to the Church, and it's better to wait until an individual is ready to make such a commitment than to force anyone to do what they aren't prepared to do.

Confirmation is sometimes referred to as "the sacrament of Christian maturity," but Christian maturity doesn't necessarily correlate with age. For example, an adult may simply never reach Christian maturity, while a child, through the workings of the Holy Spirit, may reach it quite early. The general guidelines for Confirmation is that the confirmands must have attained the age of reason, be able to profess the faith, be in a state of grace, desire the sacrament, and be prepared to assume the role of disciple and witness to Christ.

The Gifts of the Spirit

Many people associate the gifts of the Holy Spirit with the Sacrament of Confirmation. After all, the bishop recites the following words while anointing the candidate's forehead: "Be sealed with the gifts of the Holy Spirit." Actually, the gifts of the Spirit were already bestowed upon us in baptism. In Confirmation, they are activated in a special way to equip us perfectly to do the work the Lord wishes us to accomplish.

The Gifts and What They Mean

Let's first get a basic understanding of the seven gifts of the Holy Spirit and what they mean to us.

- *The gift of wisdom*. Wisdom is the first and highest gift of the Holy Spirit, because it is the perfection of faith. Wisdom gives us the desire to contemplate the things of the world and to order our relationship to the created world properly. It helps us to see God at work in people and situations around us and to value the truths of Christian belief more than the things of this world.

- *The gift of understanding*. Understanding allows us to grasp, at least in a limited way, the very essence of the truths of the Catholic Faith. With the gift of understanding, we comprehend how we need to live as a follower of Jesus Christ, regardless of the conflicting messages in our culture about the right way to live.

- *The gift of counsel or right judgment.* With the gift of right judgment, we know the difference between right and wrong, and we choose to do what is right. A person with right judgment avoids sin and lives out the values taught by Jesus, believing that the Holy Spirit will guide us in defending these truths.

- *The gift of fortitude or courage.* With the gift of courage, we overcome our fear and are willing to take risks as a follower of Jesus. A person with courage is willing to stand up for what is right in the sight of God, even if it means accepting rejection, verbal abuse, or physical harm and death.

- *The gift of knowledge.* This gift enables us to understand the meaning of God's Revelation, especially as expressed in the life and words of Jesus Christ. A person with knowledge is always learning more about the Scriptures and Tradition in order to be able to judge all things according to the truths of the Catholic faith. Through this gift of the Holy Spirit, we can determine God's purpose for our lives and live that purpose accordingly.

- *The gift of piety or reverence.* Piety is a deep sense of respect for God and the Church. A person with reverence recognizes our total reliance on God and comes before him with humility, trust, and love. Piety is the gift whereby, at the Holy Spirit's instigation, we desire and are willing to worship and serve God out of love, not duty.

- *Fear of the Lord or awe of God.* A person with this gift knows that God is the perfection of all we desire: perfect knowledge, perfect goodness, perfect power, and perfect love. Knowing that truth, we desire not to offend God out of love, as a little child fears offending his father.

Unwrapping the Gifts

It's important for every Catholic to understand the gifts of the Holy Spirit. But equally important is to understand that these gifts have to be *unwrapped*. By that I mean we have to cooperate with grace to activate these gifts in our lives. Here is an example that works well with young people. Suppose a person had two large pockets stuffed with gold coins, yet this person lived his entire life like a pauper, because he never realized he had the coins within reach of his fingertips. They just sat useless in his pockets. Would that man be considered wise? Of course not. In a similar way, we need to pray that the gifts of the Holy Spirit will be activated in our lives so that we can benefit from their riches.

Sharing the Gifts with Others

This leads into the next point, the purpose of the gifts. The gifts of the Holy Spirit are not for our own personal gain, but are meant to be shared with others. They fully enable us to do the work God has called us to, and each one of us has been called uniquely to do different work. I urge young people (as well as adults) to pray diligently to discover their special mission in life. What is it that God has uniquely equipped us to do to be his hands, feet, eyes, heart, and words on this earth? All of us have a special mission. We are all created to leave behind a treasure on this earth, a giving of ourselves that only we can give. To never discover your special purpose is to wander through life aimlessly and unhappily. Contrary to what the world may say, it is only this giving away to others, this being Christ to one another, that brings us total fulfillment and joy. Confirmation is a perfect time to inspire young people to explore their potential missions and set them on a path to lead a fulfilled adult life.

A Call to Witness and Evangelize

The Sacrament of Confirmation commissions us to go forth into the world and proclaim the Good News to those in our circle of influence (which may be much larger than you imagine at first). Specifically, the confirmand is being sent out to spread and defend the faith by word and deed. I remember this happening with our oldest son, Michael, when we moved him from Catholic school to public school so that he could take advantage of programs unavailable in our parish school. On his very first day on the public school bus, he sat behind two Baptist girls who were discussing the subject of God. Michael, uninvited but with a good heart, jumped into the conversation. The dialogue continued for weeks. Michael would come home and ask us a question about our faith, and we would give him an answer. When we weren't certain, we checked the Catechism and our collection of Catholic apologetics magazines. I'm not sure whatever happened with those girls, or if they were ever satisfied with Michael's answers, but my husband and I were both proud of our son's efforts.

In high school, Michael would bring a friend steeped in Wicca (a nature-based, New Age religion) into the Church, and today at college he continues to invite students to Mass with him. Like Michael, all of us are similarly called to share our love and knowledge of our faith—not in a superior way, but because, as I once heard a religious sister say, we are poor beggars who have stumbled upon an unbelievable treasure that we just can't keep to ourselves.

A Beginning, Not an Ending

We need a total paradigm shift in our thinking when it comes to Confirmation. It is not a graduation or an ending. It is a beginning. While the sacrament may mark the end of one form of religious education (such as CCD classes), it does not mark the end of our learning about our faith. This would be as ludicrous as saying that a wedding marks the end of a love relationship. A wedding marks the *beginning* of a new life together, a deepening of relationship. The same applies to Confirmation.

I sometimes give kids the example of an imaginary 74-year-old man who, in his youth, was baptized and confirmed in the Catholic Church. He goes on to do quite well in college, graduating at the top of his class. He lands a fabulous job, discovers the cure for cancer, gives to his community, and treats everyone fairly and with respect. He lives a good life. But if this man stopped learning and growing in his faith immediately after Confirmation, he is out of balance—he has the intelligence and social esteem of a 74-year-old man, but the faith of a fourteen-year-old. This story reminds us that our faith needs to grow right along with the rest of us.

Something We Live, Not Just Study

Why do we so often forget this need to grow in faith? A cradle-Catholic friend of mine recently opened my eyes to part of the problem. "Elizabeth," he insisted, "you don't understand. When you're raised Catholic and attend parochial school, religion is just one more subject like math or English. You write papers on it, you get tested on it, and you get homework and a grade!" This was a foreign concept for me, as I had gone to public school all my life where religion had nothing to do with my formal education. My friend's words made me take pause. How do we move past religion being treated like a school subject, something "out there" and having nothing to do with us personally?

Reflections Parents Can Make

Truly, there is no magic formula. The answer comes through actions such as prayer, study, and participation in the sacraments to allow God to do his work within us. If we've missed something in our catechesis about our faith, whether we attended Catholic school or public school, it's never too late to learn. And there's no better time or place to do that than alongside our children as they are learning. It makes the process more meaningful for everyone. The same applies to the Sacrament of Confirmation. This is an excellent time for us parents to reflect on our own Confirmation experience:

- How are we doing in fulfilling our baptismal promises and responding to the Holy Spirit?
- How are we developing our gifts?

- What gifts do we seem to have, and which ones could we pray more to activate in our life?

These are wonderful discussion points to have with your young teenager. And finally, we need to pray. Pray for and with your confirmand as he or she prepares for this amazing sacrament. Pray for your own faith, as well, and for that of your family.

Choosing a Sponsor

Another person who can play a key role in praying for the confirmand is the Confirmation sponsor. The sponsor is someone other than the parents, a person who takes his or her faith seriously and will be there for the confirmand. The sponsor will fill an important role in the life of your child, so encourage your son or daughter to choose this person wisely. (In fact, I enthusiastically suggest that you participate in that decision process!) To emphasize the unity between baptism and Confirmation, although the sacraments are separated by several years, it is entirely appropriate for the sponsor to be one of the child's baptismal godparents. Explain the purpose of the sponsor carefully to your son or daughter so that he or she can make a responsible decision.

Saints Alive!

One of my favorite parts about speaking on the Sacrament of Confirmation is re-introducing the concept of the saints. I say *re-introduce* because the saints are one of the great treasures of our Catholic faith, even though they have become largely forgotten by too many modern Catholics—and for some, a bit awkward to explain to non-Catholic friends. Saints, however, are integral to our spiritual journey. They are an important way that God shows us his love and protection. Throughout history, the Church has recognized men, women, and at times even children, from all different social classes, ethnic backgrounds, and life situations, and has held them up for our example. This was not for the benefit of the saint (because sainthood is only conferred after a person's death), but because *we* are called to be saints, too. These holy individuals were singled out due to their heroic virtue— ways they rose above and beyond great difficulties in life to hold firm to their love for God and to share that love with others through their powerful example.

Most Catholics can name at least a few of the more popular saints. But there are thousands of Church-recognized saints, each with a different story on how they triumphed over the temptations and struggles that many of us continue to face even today. Their stories and deep insight can have a profound impact on our lives and open our hearts and minds to new spiritual heights. But what surprises most Catholics I speak with is the idea that saints are not simply dead people from the past. They are *alive*, in heaven, close to our Heavenly Father, and they are waiting and desiring to intercede for us. I wonder, in this third millennium, how many of us call on these heavenly helpers. It's important to clarify here that we don't worship saints (not even the greatest saint, the Blessed Mother). We honor them and we call upon them to stand before God with our petitions. Yes, we can go directly to God with our prayers. But just as we ask for the prayers of friends and family on earth when times of difficulty arise, so can we call on the community of saints in heaven when we are in need. And they respond, according to the plan of the Father, from whom all their power comes.

My First Heavenly Helper

Like many people I meet, I have had my own experience of being blessed by the saints. My first brush with the saints happened when I was an eight-year-old Protestant, walking to public school. On the way, I happened to find a medal lying on the sidewalk. I had enough Catholic friends at the time to recognize that this was a Catholic medal. It seemed logical to me that the veiled woman on the medal, holding flowers and a cross in her arms, was the Virgin Mary. But the inscription on the back of the medal was most bewildering: *After my death I shall let fall a shower of roses.* It wouldn't be until my Catholic adulthood, as I began reading about the saints, that I correctly identified the woman on the medal as St. Thérèse of Lisieux, also known as the Little Flower. I began to have the feeling that finding the medal was not an accident at all, that somehow this saint had been sent to watch over me and that she would play an important role in my spiritual life. I would later experience blessings related to Thérèse and have the chance to correspond with others who had experienced such blessings.[4]

Resources for Growing Closer to the Saints

St. Thérèse is a one of our most dearly loved saints. Her autobiography, *Story of a Soul*, has been read by millions of people in dozens of languages. Millions more turned out to venerate her relics as they traveled the globe in the past ten years. But the Little Flower is only one of an enormous cadre of saints who can watch over us, intercede for us, and literally change our lives. Discover these wonderful examples of Christian love with your children. There are books on the saints for the youngest children, chapter books for older children to read, and a vast array of books about the saints on an adult level written by theologians, scholars, and lay authors. Even better than reading *about* the saints, read what the saints themselves wrote! Many captured their spiritual journeys, their awakenings, their lessons, and even at times their visions in precious books and letters. A few classics that come to mind are *Confessions* by St. Augustine, *Introduction to the Devout Life* by St. Francis de Sales, *The Spiritual Exercises by* St. Ignatius of Loyola, *The Dialogue* by St. Catherine of Sienna, *The Interior Castle* by St. Teresa of Avila, *Story of a Soul* by St. Thérèse of Lisieux, and *Dark Night of the Soul* by St. John of the Cross.

Choosing a Confirmation Name

Raising our children with a good knowledge of the saints is an important faith experience for the entire family. Use a "saint of the day" book to foster mealtime discussion or focus on the saints listed on the liturgical calendar. Remind children that when they reach Confirmation age, they will be asked to select the name of a saint who will accompany them for life, and invite them to begin thinking about this important and personal decision now. The name should not be chosen because it sounds nice, or because a friend has selected it, but because it represents a saint the young person can relate to or wishes to emulate. If an eighth grader has no previous knowledge of the saints when he or she is asked to select a Confirmation name, this process can become a chore and a drudge instead of an exciting and rewarding adventure of choosing a special saint partner for life, so make the saints part of your daily home life long before Confirmation time.

Choosing a "Saint for a Year"

One of the ways my husband and I make the subject of saints come alive in our family is through a tradition we picked up from another family called "Saint for the Year." It goes like this. First, find a comprehensive list of saints (there are many good ones online). Cut the names into little slips of paper and place them in an envelope. Gather your family together and offer a prayer to the Holy Spirit, then pass the envelope around and have each family member select one. This becomes your saint for the year. (You can also choose names randomly from a good book of saints.) The purpose of this exercise is threefold. First, you are to learn about your saint. Some saints are quite familiar, such as St. Francis or St. Patrick, but others are more obscure and perhaps even completely unknown. Therefore, do some research on your saint to discover when this person lived and what he or she did to warrant the title of saint. Second, incorporate your saint into your prayer life for the upcoming year. When life is difficult or you are celebrating a particular joy, bring your saint into that situation. Third, and most important, try and discern why the Holy Spirit connected you with this particular saint for this particular year of your life. The revelations can be fascinating.

The following year, gather your family again and share a little about your saint for the benefit of the others and tell them about your spiritual journey with that individual. Then, choose a new saint for the upcoming year. We began this tradition several years ago with my husband's extended family. We used Christmas as a time to select a new saint. More recently, we've moved this tradition from Christmas to All Saints Day, as a way to put more emphasis on that Feast Day that can often get overshadowed by the distractions of Halloween. We've also gotten into the practice of using email to share insights with the family during the year, instead of waiting until our annual get-together.

The first year we did this tradition in our family, I received the name of St. John the Baptist. This happened to be the year I began doing public speaking in addition to my writing ministry, and I called upon my saint often that year for strength and encouragement, since the Baptist was certainly known to be a dynamic speaker. Another year, I received the name of a lesser-known saint, St. Louise de Marillac. In my research, I learned she was affiliated with St. Vincent de Paul and founded the Daughters of Charity in Paris. I couldn't imagine the significance of this French nun in my life, until a few months later when I was sent to France to work on a book about Lourdes. A small group of us had an opportunity to spend an afternoon in Paris on the way home, and we found ourselves at Rue du Bac, site of the famous apparitions of St. Catherine Laboure and the message of the Miraculous Medal. As I visited this convent, my jaw dropped when I came upon a statue of St. Louise de Marillac. She had been Catherine's mother superior! I actually prayed on her gravesite, marveling at the workings of Holy Spirit.

The Saint for the Year tradition is one I've also suggested to teachers for use in their classroom. If you are a teacher, ask your students to do the same three steps:

1. Learn about their saint
2. Incorporate their saint into their prayer life
3. See if there isn't some significance to having drawn that saint's name that particular year.

This simple activity can really plant the seeds for a lifetime of love and appreciation for the saints.

Life After Confirmation

As we noted earlier in this chapter, Confirmation is not an ending, but a beginning. These young confirmands are about to enter the most challenging decade of their lives, as temptations and distractions in high school and college will battle fiercely to pull them off their paths to holiness. It's absolutely critical to establish a sense of belonging in these young people—belonging not just to the parish, but to the universal Church. They need to see themselves as an integral part of a bigger picture—as members of the community—or the risk is great that they will eventually drift away. A loving Christian community helps to offset the constant challenge to fit in or buckle under the peer pressure of adolescence. This is a time the Confirmation sponsor can play a pivotal role—but not if he or she is struggling with the same issues. Again, choose the sponsor wisely, one who will set a good example and be there for the young person in his or her developments and struggles.

The Importance of Youth Ministry

A vibrant youth ministry program is a terrific way for young people to find like-minded peers and be somewhat buffeted against dangerous trends in our modern culture. The purpose of such a ministry is to help keep young people connected to God and their parish. A good youth ministry program should be kid-friendly and offer age-appropriate fun activities, but never at the expense of serving its primary purpose: to nurture spiritual development in Catholic teens. There are a number of popular and engaging Catholic speakers who offer books and videos specifically geared to Catholic teens and young adults that can be incorporated into a youth ministry program: Jason Evert, Justin Fatica, Steve Angrisandro, Chris Padgett, Jesse Romero, and Matthew Kelly are just a few examples.

Does a youth ministry program necessarily *have* to be Catholic, I'm often asked? Ultimately, yes. Even though the exciting youth program at the church down the street may be fun, social, prayerful, and filled with nice young men and women, it cannot feed our Catholic youth with the sacraments. I cannot underscore enough the importance of inflaming young hearts with the reality of Jesus in the Eucharist and Reconciliation. As we've read in previous chapters, these are powerful sacraments that help us discern our purpose, fortify us against temptation, and inspire our passion for holiness. Because of the difficult and dangerous times in which we live, including the high rate of suicide among teenagers, the sacraments can literally be life-saving for some individuals. So for Catholic youth, I strongly recommend authentically Catholic youth programs.

Youth Masses provide a means of reaching out to young people through music and youth participation. Catholic praise and worship experiences are growing in popularity, incorporating popular Christian music with lyrics that at times are surprisingly Catholic. Within our diocese, we have "Jesus Jams," a monthly event that attracts hundreds of youth in the area with Mass, praise and worship, a dynamic speaker, youth testimonials, raucous skits, and an opportunity for making a Confession. On a larger scale are youth conventions such as the National Catholic Youth Conference (NCYC) that travel around the country, bringing thousands of on-fire Catholic youth together, or on an even grander scale, World Youth Day, which attracts hundreds of thousands. Experiences like these make lasting impressions on both the youth and the adults who chaperone them. Find out what the opportunities are in your area, or create one of your own!

Getting Young People Involved in Parish Ministry

Here's a final idea I've presented to DREs for keeping young people involved in their parish after Confirmation. In the beginning of the Confirmation year, invite representatives from each of your parish ministries (such as food pantry, pro-life, funeral support, altar society, sick and shut-in, hospitality, music, prayer groups, and adoration) to come in and give a five-minute talk on what their particular ministry entails, the joys of serving in this capacity, and perhaps an interesting story. Have each confirmand select a ministry he or she will commit to getting involved in that year. At the end of the year, have a party with snacks and invite parents to attend. Go around the room and allow the young people to share their experiences of working in these various ministries. The idea is that they will be inspired to stay in the ministry longer, or perhaps switch to another ministry based on their peers' feedback. At the very least, awareness will be increased among these young people regarding the ministries available at your particular parish. It's a useful way to increase the likelihood that they will get involved and stay connected. And be sure to have the most enthusiastic student participants talk about their positive experiences with the *next* class of confirmands.

Looking Ahead...

In this chapter, we learned that Confirmation in the Catholic faith involves a conferring of grace by the Holy Spirit that empowers us to spread and defend the faith by word and deed. Receiving this sacrament is a serious commitment because it is a call to witness and evangelize. We've looked at the gifts of the Holy Spirit, and how they are meant to be used and shared with others. We've learned how we can help our young people embrace this sacrament through careful discernment of a Confirmation sponsor and Confirmation name and by turning to the saints for help and encouragement. We concluded with ways that young people can stay active in their parishes, transforming them into faithful Catholic adults ready to discern their vocation in life. Could this vocation be marriage? We'll look at that sacrament next.

5

REFLECTION OF GOD'S LOVE

The Sacrament of Matrimony

From Genesis to Revelation, Holy Scripture teems with evidence that marriage is a vital plan and design of God. In the creation story, God saw that it was not good for man to be alone. Therefore, he created woman so that the two would be a source of help, consolation, and joy for one another. God created man and woman in his likeness (an image of love) and willed that the two would be together always in a new and intimate expression of existence. *"Therefore a man leaves his father and his mother and cleaves to his wife, and they become one flesh"* (Gen 2:24). At the center of this first happy union was the welcomed presence of God until, as the story goes, Adam and Eve were unfaithful to their Creator and sin and discord entered the world. Despite this unfaithfulness, the story illustrates God's original design of a unique love between human and Divine.

We see the concept of a committed fidelity attempted again and again throughout the Old Testament in the form of God's holy covenant with his people, Israel. While the Israelites were often unfaithful to God as they tested him and turned to false idols, God's love and loyalty for his chosen ones never faltered. The coming of Jesus—which embodies an even greater bond of intimacy between God and his people—and the repeated references to Christ as groom, and the Church as bride, make clear that marriage is of great importance to our Heavenly Father. Jesus could have come into the world in any number of ways. He could have hatched from an egg or been beamed down in a spaceship. Instead, God willed that the Incarnate Word would enter the world through a human family and be nurtured within the marital bonds of his loving earthly parents.

The fact that Jesus' first public miracle takes place at the celebration of a marriage also says a great deal about how important this sacred union is in God's eyes. Jesus blesses the couple and the event at Cana, showing that it is good by turning water into choice wine. In this action, he demonstrates his power over nature and marks the beginning of his public ministry. The miracle (as we said earlier) prefigures the changing of wine into the blood of the new covenant Jesus will form with his people. Through his powerful presence and this miraculous action, marriage is transformed into something much deeper than a natural institution. Holy Scripture concludes its marital theme with an elaborate description of the heavenly wedding banquet that God yearns to celebrate with each of us for all eternity (Revelation 19). As we can see, marriage is an eternal concept of which God is the true author.

More than a Piece of Paper

St. Augustine, sometime in the late fourth century, was the first Church father to speak of marriage as having sacramental qualities. But it would not be until the Council of Trent (1545–1563), in answer to Protestant opposition, that the Church would formally reaffirm the sacramentality and indissolubility of marriage. The Church had come to recognize that baptized Christians were transformed by the Holy Spirit into new creations in Christ, healed from original sin, and invited to share in the divine life. Therefore, Christ's saving action elevated and perfected the marital union between baptized Christians to be a reflection of the total gift of self-love of Christ for his Church. It was an outward sign instituted by Christ to give grace, which is the definition of sacrament.

Granted, it took a while for the Church to work out all the details about marriage, particularly regarding the marital act. While the Church always saw the goodness of sex within a marriage for procreative purposes, it took longer to fully understand and embrace the *unitive* (or bonding) purposes of sexual relations between a husband and wife. We are fortunate today to live in an era of heightened awareness of and appreciation for the sanctity of marital love. Vatican II marked a positive turn toward accepting human sexuality as a gift of the Creator. With the Council's document *Gaudium et Spes* ("The Church in the Modern World"), the Church for the first time placed the good of the couple on equal footing with procreation.

Pope John Paul II further explored the gift and beauty of human sexuality, particularly as it pertains to married couples, in a series of Wednesday audiences he gave between 1979 and 1984. These insightful lectures, an integrated vision of the human person—body, soul, and spirit—were compiled into a work called *Theology of the Body*. It is, as Catholic theologian and commentator George Weigel describes in his papal biography, *Witness to Hope*, "one of the boldest reconfigurations of Catholic theology in centuries… a kind of theological time bomb set to go off with dramatic consequences, sometime in the third millennium of the Church." (pp. 336, 343)

My Own Marriage as Sacrament

Reading about the history of the Catholic Church as it wrestled over the centuries to grasp and convey the full meaning and beauty of marriage, I take some solace in the fact that it has taken nearly twenty-five years for my husband and I to begin to understand our own marriage as sacrament. After dating for five years, we were married in a small Italian parish in Raritan, New Jersey. It was a pretty setting for a wedding, with warm mahogany accents, ornate stained glass windows and murals, and lots of flowers. Our bridal party, decked in complementary dusty rose dresses and light grey suits, consisted of siblings, cousins, and friends. We invited the priest who had given us our Engaged Encounter Weekend to marry us, and his homily on marriage was inspiring. The ceremony was followed by a lovely 12-hour backyard reception at my in-law's home. On that beautiful summer day, I had only one thought in mind: finally, after years of waiting, I was marrying my best friend. No longer would we have to commute from different states to see one another. Our new life together was about to begin, and the word *together* had a very nice ring to it!

Reflecting on our engagement and wedding, I realize how little my husband and I had understood then about the Catholic perspective on marriage. Yes, it was for a lifetime, and yes, we needed to be open to children and committed to bringing them up in the faith. But we were oblivious to the concept of marriage *as a sacrament*. We thought, as most couples do, that the priest who married us had the power to magically make us united with his ritualistic words and actions. We didn't realize that it was the two of us who were marrying each other—that *we* were the primary ministers of the sacrament. (The Church teaches that the priest—or in some cases, the deacon—is actually there to assist at the celebration and receive the couple's consent in the name of the Church and give them the Church's blessing.) Most of all, we did not fully appreciate the special bond being formed not just between the two of us, but between us and our Creator, and what that would mean for the rest of our married life.

God's Strengthening Presence

As we've been discussing throughout this book, sacraments reveal God's special presence in a powerful and intimate way. That means God is present in our Catholic marriages, too. I've always been comfortable with the concept of God as the third person in our marriage, but to contemplate him present in our marital bond, alive and sacred as he is in Confession or in the Eucharist, is something quite different. His presence means there is strength in our unity. It means we have been given the grace to live marriage and withstand the inevitable bumps that will come our way. His presence enables us to pick up our crosses and follow him, to rise when we've fallen, to forgive one another and bear one another's burdens. Everything we need to survive and flourish is already contained within the marriage sacrament. But it doesn't happen without any participation on our part. Just like in the example we saw of the person with the pockets full of gold coins, we need to unwrap the gifts of the sacrament, digging down and calling upon those graces of God regularly to get us through each day of married life, through all the little things, so they don't grow into even bigger problems tomorrow. Our marital bond is like a font we must return to, over and over again, for replenishment.

The Desperate Need for Sacramental Marriage

At its best, marriage is a lifelong partnership of mutual fidelity and love. It is a sacred union that encourages a couple to grow in virtue and holiness by presenting them with continual opportunities to overcome selfishness and become self-giving for the good of the family. Ideally in marriage, we learn to see our spouses through the eyes of God, and we strive to mirror God's love back to one another, making visible to all the image of God's love. In living the sacrament, our focus is not only to love, honor, and cherish one another—it is to help our spouse journey to heaven. The love between a married couple—enhanced by their love for God—is powerful and contagious. It extends beyond the couple to touch family and community in life-giving ways.

Unfortunately, marriage is not always experienced at its best. In fact, we may be living in one of the most challenging times in history as far as marital success and happiness are concerned. The statistics are gloomy. According to data issued by the U.S. Council of Catholic Bishops, the number of couples approaching the Church for a sacramental wedding has decreased by 48% in the past three decades. Many young Catholics are getting married in other churches or obtaining a secular marriage through a justice of the peace. Among those who do get married, nearly half of all marriages end in divorce. And more and more couples – over five million—choose cohabitation in lieu of marriage. But this arrangement, as we will see, does little to ensure happily-ever-afters.

A contraceptive mentality has become widespread among Catholics in their childbearing years, even among those who are married. But as Pope Paul VI predicted in his 1968 encyclical *Humanae Vitae,* separating the unitive and procreative functions of marriage could damage or destroy it and have negative effects personally and socially. Specifically, he foretold that contraception would lead to marital infidelity, a moral decline, a loss of respect of women, an abuse of power (such as forced abortion in Third World countries), and the mistaken notion that man had unlimited dominion over his own body; this would open the door to further problems such as sterilization, euthanasia, and test tube babies. While Pope Paul's gloomy prophecies were widely rejected at the time by many lay Catholics, who were confident that the contraceptive pill was the answer to so many of their woes, the late pontiff's vision has unfortunately proven accurate. And perhaps no one has been more negatively affected than children. Today, children are no longer seen as the supreme gift of marriage or even as something integral to the sacrament, but rather as a personal option or even a commodity. The decision to have children has been disconnected from marriage. An estimated forty percent of children are born in this country without the benefit of an intact family consisting of a married mother and father, and studies show this is not in the best interest of the child.

Modeling a Good Marriage for Our Children

As parents, we are the primary teachers and catechists for our children. Since they learn more through what we do than what we say, how we live our relationship (whether in marriage or divorce) is going to send them a powerful message that will affect their foundational attitudes on relationship.

Before we talk about marriage, let's address the situation of divorce, since it is as prevalent today in Catholic households as it is outside of the Church. If you are among the divorced population, and rectifying the marriage is no longer possible, the Church expects that you will live a chaste life and seek annulment options before entering into another marriage. Even though marriage may not have worked out well for you, I'm sure as a parent you want better for your children. You don't want them to go through the disillusionment and disappointment that you've experienced. While it may be hard, resist the temptation to speak bitterly with your children about your former relationship and instead communicate to them God's vision for marriage: a loving bond for a lifetime. Regrettably, sometimes things don't work out the way we would have liked. We have to acknowledge the degree to which our generation allowed ourselves to be more influenced by the culture than by our faith. Many of us entered into marital relationships without sufficient discernment and preparation and without a concerted effort to keep God at the center. While *we* may have missed this important lesson, we can still teach it to our children. They need to know that, whatever our own experiences, happy marriages *are* possible today. It will take good knowledge of self, a clear definition of expectations, a careful discernment of the choice of partner, a willingness to be self-giving, and a commitment to place faith in the center of one's life.

To be of service to our children, we must be the voice of reason, especially in a world in which reason seems to have become a lost art. That means speaking out clearly against issues that are contrary to our faith and living an upright life ourselves. I'm not sure if some parents today are afraid of being disliked by their children or if they lack the vision to see the long-term consequences of a given situation, but I'm often startled by the permissiveness I see in many families. All young people yearn for structure, leadership, and direction, even though they don't act like it and will often rebel. That's their way of testing the stability of the structure and making sure it's solid.

When the US bishops surveyed young people about their attitudes regarding marriage, they found them fearful of getting hurt and ill-equipped to sacrifice for others. These young people have grown up in a world that has repeatedly let them down with its lies and illusions. They have had their trust broken by people in the limelight as well as people in their own families. Naturally, they are leery about trusting others, particularly in a commitment as serious as marriage. For all the electronic communication young people engage in currently, and for all the increased sexual activity, their connection with others remains on a surface level without any sense of intimacy, a revealing of who they truly are at their inmost core to another person. As parents trying to model marriage as a sacrament, we need to give young people a message that flies in the face of what they're hearing from the culture, one that celebrates the dignity of married love and the value of chastity. And we need to deliver that message when they are young children, still open to the wisdom of their parents and not so influenced by raging hormones and romantic feelings.

Offering a Message for Children and Young People

As I talk about strategies we can use to teach our children about marriage, keep in mind that the young people in your circle of influence are not limited to your sons and daughters. You can use these ideas with grandchildren, nieces and nephews, godchildren, or students you teach in a religion class.

While marriage may be a long way off for young children, it's never too early to start teaching them about this sacrament, which statistically will likely be a part of their future lives. Children are already forming their ideas and opinions about marriage through their experiences in their own families, their friends' families, and by what is portrayed in media and entertainment. Early education on the sacrament of marriage is key!

Begin by teaching children that marriage is a serious commitment that must be entered into carefully. The choice of a spouse is enormously significant to the rest of their lives. Most of all, explain that marriage is a sacrament, not just a piece of paper, and what that sacrament means to us as Catholics. (This is where you want to begin planting seeds that it really does make a difference as to what church a person gets married in, and how their future marriage will get off on the best foot possible with the graces of a Catholic wedding.) Communicate to your children that despite the grim realities of our world today, divorce and separation are not God's plan for us. God wants husbands and wives to stay together and to raise their children in an intact family. We increase the chance of our children attaining a strong marriage by our example of keeping God in the center of our relationship and drawing on him constantly for support.

Encourage your children, particularly those approaching their teen years, to begin praying early to discern which vocation they are being called to: the single life, the religious life, or the married life. Urge them to ask God this question regularly. If they think they are being called to the married state one day, have them begin praying for their future spouse *now*.

At first, this may seem a bit odd, but I've presented it this way when I'm speaking to young people. I select a strong, handsome-looking young man from the audience and ask him if he thinks one day he'll get married. After a few embarrassed giggles, the answer is typically *yes*. I then propose to the young man that his future spouse is out there, somewhere, right now. Perhaps he's already met her. More likely, he hasn't. I ask the young man to imagine what his future wife is doing right now. Perhaps she's studying for a big test. Great. Maybe she's texting a girlfriend. Okay. Then I look the young man directly in the eye and suggest that maybe his future spouse is on a date right now at a drive-in movie with the quarterback of the football team. The young man begins to squirm. This, I explain to the audience, is why we want to get our young people in the habit of praying for our future spouse *now*. We want that individual to be safe. We don't want him or her to be drinking, drugging, sleeping around, or hurting him or herself in any way. At the same time, we also don't want to hurt *ourselves*, because we have a responsibility to our future spouse. "The choices you make now as unmarried singles," I tell young people, "can end up haunting you for a lifetime. Ask God constantly to help you stay on your path to holiness."

We will do a great service to our young people if we can talk to them early on about the advantages of taking it slow and making careful decisions that reflect their values so they don't end up giving up their options in life already by the time they're 20. Our goal is to prepare our children with solid teaching about God's plan for relationships now so they can one day engage in an honorable courtship and marriage of their own.

Preparing Grown Children
for the Sacrament of Marriage

As children grow into adulthood, outside influences grow, too. Good Catholic parents are understandably disheartened when their grown children stop going to church and move in with someone out of wedlock. Studies done by the Center for Marital and Family Studies at the University of Denver show that people want the security and lifelong love that marriage offers, but they are very fearful about obtaining this. Young adults have widely bought into the notion that living with someone prior to marriage is a great way to test the relationship and see how well the two people can get along in the same living space. Studies, however, indicate quite the opposite. Living together before marriage actually *reduces* the chance of martial success.

The Center, through a federally funded program, has been looking closely at cohabitation and its long-term effects on the participants. It has found that most couples enter into cohabiting without a great deal of discussion or discernment. Perhaps one person spends a night at the other's apartment, then two, then three. Or perhaps one of the partners has a lease that's about to expire and moving in together sort of "happens" without much sense of commitment and goal setting from either person. It has also been proven that living together makes it harder to break up with a person than when not living together. If the cohabiting couple decides eventually to marry, it may have more to do with a child that has entered the picture rather than a deep commitment and passion and a sense of knowing that "this is the right person for me." Studies also show that males are significantly less dedicated to their mates after marriage if they've lived together prior to getting married. Finally, for couples who cohabit without any intention of getting married, the breakup rate is as high as the divorce rate among married couples and, in some reports, even higher.

Ask Questions about Choices

Here is a question worth asking couples who are considering cohabitation: Have you given any thought to the fact that it's harder to break up when you are living with someone than when you are not? That once you move in with someone you might end up marrying that person only because it was harder to break up than to marry? Do you see how this decision can lead you to make the wrong choice of partner and give up your options later? Young adults may not initially see the risk of cohabiting, but they do understand the concept of options and choices, and this approach may get them to think about their decision more deeply.

The Lost Art of Courtship

A currently popular book and movie series is *Twilight*, the romantic adventure between a girl and her vampire boyfriend. While the series has messages and a dark side that I find particularly troublesome, its wild popularity among young girls *and* their mothers is interesting and worth examining. I think what really stokes feminine interest in the series is the concept of *courtship*: a yearning for someone you can't have right now, a desire to attract the long-term interest of another, and the importance of taking things slow. We are all created for love and courtship. We are designed to be attracted to others and to be the apple of someone's eye. That's all good and beautiful. But somewhere along the way, we have lost the art of courtship. Relationships too often progress at lightning speed and skip all the important steps of getting to know one another: our expectations, our fears, our dreams and desires. A good question to pose to our children who are dating is this: "Is my involvement with this person going to make me a better individual?" Our children today need coaching on the purpose and value of courtship and dating (as do many of us adults), and that is an excellent first step to marriage preparation.

Moving from Me to We

Another relationship aspect we want to prepare young adults for as they contemplate marriage is *forgiveness* and *reconciliation*. In marriage we are called to heal the hurts, large and small, that can regularly come between spouses. We need to understand ourselves and the shortcomings we bring to the relationship and be willing to confess our faults to our partner without blame or excuses. In seeking healing, it's not enough to say "I'm sorry." A more appropriate statement, because it requires a response from the offended party, is "Please forgive me." Since our culture is one that skirts the issues of sin, right and wrong, and even basic accountability, young adults are often ill-prepared to understand the value of forgiveness in terms of building trust and intimacy between one another. This must be an important part of their marriage preparation.

By the time young adults are preparing to approach the altar, they have probably established a deep sense of individualism. This is a strong value in society today. There is great emphasis placed on what *I* want, what *I* need, and what *I* think. However, there's no room for this kind of individualism within a marriage. It's not that marriage requires us to lose our identities altogether; each of us will always be a unique personality within our relationship. But the focus in marriage necessarily changes from "me" to "we," with the bottom line always being what is the best for our relationship and our family. Furthermore, in a sacramental marriage, we are called to die to self so that we can bring life to one another. This is an unconditional commitment that many people are afraid to make today. It's why we see the growing trend of cohabitation, prolonged engagements, and even co-ownership on major investments like land and houses, all in the hope of trying to make the union more secure.

The exaggerated notion of individualism prevents most couples from understanding that marriage is not a private affair, but something meant for the common good of society. Our sacrament is supposed to reflect Christ's love for his Church, and that's a serious responsibility. In the same way, a broken marriage, too, is not a private affair that affects only the immediate family members. It means there is one less reflection of Christ's love for his Church, and that hurts all of us in the long run.

Nurturing Existing Marriages

So what can we do to protect and nurture our marriages, so they can be an important reflection of Christ's love to a hurting world? Society is certainly not doing much to promote healthy marriages. Instead, the sacred union between a husband and wife is often devalued in television, movies, books, and the news. Marriage today is no longer seen as a received truth from God regarding the complementarity of man and woman, but as something that can be redefined based on fleeting political interests.

Even if society were more supportive, however, marriage is still hard work, and it requires a great deal of nourishment. For two people with different personalities and interests to spend their life together harmoniously, it takes sacrifice, humility, honesty, and persistence. For two people to nurture and sustain a sacrament, it takes obedience to God's will. As marriage becomes a topic of greater concern to our bishops, more parishes are implementing formal marriage enrichment programs for their congregations. These are an excellent way to care for your marriage. Faith sharing groups consisting of married couples, in which small groups of parishioners can share their struggles and victories in family life, are also an effective source of support. A mentoring program that involves connecting newlyweds with seasoned married couples is yet another effective way to support marriages within the parish.

Worldwide Marriage Encounter

In the summer of 2009, Stanislaw Cardinal Rylko, President of the Pontifical Council for the Laity, and Ennio Cardinal Antonelli, President of the Pontifical Council for the Family, met with the leadership of Worldwide Marriage Encounter to seek a more formal relationship with the Vatican. The Worldwide Marriage Encounter movement, active in over 90 countries, has been enriching marriages for more than forty years. An estimated five million couples and tens of thousands of priests have made a Marriage Encounter Weekend. This unique experience revitalizes marriages that have experienced disillusionment (which is, technically, *all* marriages at one point or another) by giving couples a special tool of communication that enables them to rebuild their intimacy, trust, and affection for one another. Couples married five years or fifty find themselves falling in love with each other all over again after making a Weekend. It is literally a life-changing experience.

Why do priests make a Marriage Encounter Weekend? The priest is espoused to his people, the Church. To live his sacrament of Holy Orders to the fullest, he is called to engage with his people with a sense of trust and vulnerability similar to what is required by married couples. Priests that have made a Weekend find themselves rejuvenated in their vocation, with a greater appreciation for their married laity and an effective tool to offer those who are striving to make their marriages better.

My husband and I made a Marriage Encounter Weekend a number of years ago, and it was the best thing we ever did for our sacrament. Our communication, intimacy, and trust were greatly enhanced to the point that even our children could see an immediate difference in our interaction. Our Weekend experience was so life-changing, we have been inspired to continue living the dream of this movement of transforming the world and the Church, one couple at a time, by becoming a presenting couple. Twice a year, we give the Weekend experience to twenty-five other couples who are looking to make their marriages better.

For couples that have been stuck in disillusionment for a long period of time and have significant difficulties in their marriages, there is another program, called Retrouvaille. It has been known to provide effective marriage help for struggling couples—even those who have separated or divorced. Currently, Retrouvaille and Marriage Encounter operate independently of the Church, but there may be a time in the not-so-distant future when these vital marriage support systems become an official outreach program in each diocese.

A Path to Holiness

The late Pope John Paul II recognized the importance of love, marriage, and family life and made this the subject of many of his addresses and writings. Although he lost his own mother when he was a young child, he clearly understood the power and protection of strong and faith-filled parenting, often citing the example of the Holy Family as a role model for Christian families. He was also instrumental in the beatification of Luigi and Maria Beltrame Quattrocchi, the first husband and wife to be beatified as a married couple. (Other married persons have been beatified and canonized in history, but not in conjunction with their spouse.) The pope cited this faithful Italian couple, who had overcome great hardships in their fifty years of marriage, as a model for all married couples. They had demonstrated the Eucharistic nature of married life—to be blessed, broken, and shared as the Body of Christ for one another. Their beatification demonstrates that the sacrament of marriage is a valid pathway toward heroic sanctity, a pathway all of us as married couples are invited to walk.

Looking Ahead…

As some factions of modern society wrestle to define marriage, the Catholic Church continues to teach that marriage is an inherent plan of God, the author of life, from the beginning of creation. In this chapter, we have learned that Catholic marriage is not just a piece of paper or an exchange of words. It is a sacrament, a living encounter with Christ, that provides strength and healing for the spouses. Considering the high rate of failed marriages (or the avoidance of marriages), we need ways to nurture our own marital bond and reveal God's plan for marriage and family in life-giving ways to our children. As we've learned, it's wise to plant these seeds early. Marriage, however, isn't the only sacramental vocation our children may be called to. Some may receive a different kind of calling, as we'll discuss in the next chapter.

6

CALLED TO SERVE

The Sacrament of Holy Orders

Jesus Christ made it abundantly clear in Scripture that in order to truly follow him, we are called to serve one another. Nowhere was this message more poignantly communicated than when the King of Kings stooped down to wash the feet of his Apostles at the Last Supper. This humble gesture of service reminds us that all Christians are called to use their gifts for the good of the community. But some individuals are called to an even deeper level of service through a consecrated life as a priest, deacon, or religious sister or brother. The Sacrament of Holy Orders pertains specifically to bishops, priests, and deacons, but for the purpose of this book, which is to foster the awareness of and appreciation for the sacramental life in families, I am going to broaden the discussion of Holy Orders to include our religious sisters and brothers, as there are wonderful opportunities for families to expose their children to all of these various religious vocations.

A religious calling can come at any time in life, and a number of adults today are surprised to find themselves experiencing the call to be a priest, deacon, brother, or sister after many years in a professional career. For others, however, the call can come early, so it's important that we open the minds and hearts of our young children to the possibilities of God's plan. What my husband and I have been telling our children through the years is that the bottom line is they are *all* being called to serve God in some capacity; it is their responsibility to discover how they are being called to carry out that service. This requires an active line of communication with God to discern the direction that he is leading, whether it's the married life, the single life, or the religious life. Our perfect happiness and fulfillment come when we are living God's will for us. For one person, that may be to live in a bustling household raising thirteen children. For another, it may be to experience the solitude of a monastery. When we follow God's direction for our lives and apply the gifts and talents he has perfectly equipped us with, our reward will be great on earth and in heaven.

"I Want to be a Nun"

I remember as a small child living near an orphanage called St. Mary's of the Angels run by the Sisters of Mercy. We would drive by it several times a month on the way home from my grandparents' house. Often, I would peer out the car window at the fully habited sisters walking the grounds with their veils and rosary beads blowing in the wind. It was like a scene out of *The Sound of Music*, one of my favorite musicals, and it even inspired me, along with some friends, to spend one summer making grandiose plans to perform our own rendition of this lovely story. I was to play the Mother Superior. Our creative plans never came to fruition, however. Our theatrical staff was quite disappointed when we approached the sisters to see if they would lend us some "costumes" for the play and we were politely turned down. We turned our creative talents to other uses that summer, like monkey bar competitions and selling lemonade.

Perhaps the most poignant memory of that orphanage was the time I announced during one of our family drives past St. Mary's that I thought one day *I* would like to be a nun. There were a few problems with my declaration, however. For starters, our family wasn't Catholic. Secondly, my parents didn't even *like* Catholics. Therefore I was chastised for making such an outlandish comment, and I made a mental note never to mention it again.

As an adult Catholic convert, I have sometimes looked back at that situation and wondered if I missed a sign that God was trying to give me. Was I supposed to have been a religious? Or was I just experiencing an early attraction to things that were Catholic? I talked about this with my pastor in Confession. At the time, there was a small group of sisters that had been attending daily Mass with us, and I couldn't help but watch them in their neat habits, their faces glowing as they participated in the liturgy. Again that little voice nagged me; *did I make the right decision?* My eyes would go from them to the infant lying on my lap and staring up at me with a big milky grin.

When I spoke with my pastor about my attraction to the sisters (along with the story of the orphanage), his answer was simple and surprising. "Elizabeth," he said, "don't you think those sisters sitting in Mass look at you with that baby in your arms and ask themselves the same question?" That thought had never occurred to me. It was a liberating moment for me that my questioning was normal, and I confidently put to rest any thoughts of being in the wrong line of work. God has placed me exactly where I need to be to complete my salvation on this earth, and all I need to concern myself with is performing that role to the best of my ability.

In my speaking and writing experience, I have come to realize that I have not been alone in questioning my vocation. This turns out to be a common question among laypeople, whether it's about being a religious or taking a different direction as a layperson. Discernment takes prayer – lots of prayer – and seeking the counsel of priests, sisters, family members, and other people we can trust. We need to trust that if God is calling us, we will get the message.

Exposing Young Children to the Religious Life

There was a time in history when most Catholic families in the U.S. and Europe would have been delighted for one or more of their children to enter into religious life. It was seen as a respectable vocation—a step up, if you will—much the way it is regarded today in Third World countries where religious vocations are booming. But in modern American and European families, there seems to be less support from parents for the idea of religious vocations for their offspring. In the past several decades, with the emphasis on materialism, consumerism, and individualism, the lure of climbing the corporate ladder and achieving an affluent way of life has taken precedence over the role of service to others. Many parents have become lukewarm in their faith and naturally produce children who are lukewarm as well. Family sizes are smaller today, too, and perhaps some parents are concerned about their lineage dying out or losing contact with a son or daughter if he or she chooses missionary work or a cloistered lifestyle. All of these factors have contributed to our current shortage of priests and religious.

It's not that God has stopped calling laborers to the harvest; it's that fewer people seem to be listening and responding. (Our current electronic age, which plugs people's ears with iPods® and Blackberries®, isn't helping the situation.) But as we discussed earlier, if we pursue our own selfish desires without any regard for God's will for our lives, we will end up feeling empty, disappointed, and unfulfilled. When we put this into perspective, we realize as parents that our role is not to steer our children into a career because *we* want it. Nor should we let them go off willy-nilly without any input on our part. Rather, we will best serve our children by guiding them to seek ways to use their God-given gifts to serve others and help usher in the Kingdom of God.

Therefore, the first thing we can do for our children is to expose them to the many ways we can serve God through vocations and occupations. We want to encourage our children early on to pray for God's guidance, to ask him for the wisdom to recognize a call *and* for the courage to follow it. I once asked a priest how to best open my sons' hearts and minds to the possibility of the priesthood. He encouraged me to have them practice being life-giving to others. This seemed to be good advice. Certainly, society wasn't going to teach them that lesson—it was up to our family to instill that at home.

In addition to having young people pray for their own vocation, we can invite them to pray with the entire family for those who are already in a religious vocation or those currently discerning one. The evil one has seemed to launch a full-blown attack on the priesthood and religious life, so our prayers are desperately needed. As I write this book, it is the Year of the Priest, and I see many parishes responding to that in creative ways. But *every* year can and should be the year of the priest and religious. Whether they are in discernment, formation, active service, or retirement, these holy men and women need and deserve our prayerful support and encouragement.

Forging Friendships

The current shortage of priests and religious can result in our children having less exposure to them. This is an unfortunate reality. Still, it is important to seek ways to try to develop friendships with those men and women of God who are in your parish or community. Try some of the following suggestions to help your entire family experience the person behind the vocation:

- Ask them about their vocation. How long have they served the church? When did they experience their first calling to religious life? What can we do to better hear the call of God in our own hearts?
- Invite them to your home for dinner. (Make it a social event, not a business meeting to discuss changes you'd like to see in your parish. This is a time for them to relax!)
- Invite them into your parochial classrooms to speak with students.

- Ask if there is something they need, or a way in which your family can help them.

The friendships our family has formed with priests, deacons, and religious sisters and brothers over the years have been a tremendous blessing to all of us. And I know they have come to deeply appreciate it, too.

Serving on the Altar

I can't think of a better way for our children to get to know priests and deacons than to serve alongside of these men on the altar during Mass. The role of altar server was traditionally reserved for young males as a way to expose and inspire them to religious life. But in 1994, Pope John Paul II made it possible for females to serve in this capacity, at the discretion of the local bishop. All four of our sons have now been trained as altar servers, and with each passing year I see them growing into their roles in terms of reverence and responsibility. They've served at Sunday Mass in addition to First Holy Communion liturgies and funerals. As I've stated earlier, our family has found that active participation in the Mass, whether it is as an altar server or a singer or musician, or simply bringing up the gifts, helps our children be more engaged in what is going on around them.

Overcoming Reluctance

I want to address briefly the reluctance some families may have in developing personal relationships with priests and religious because of newspaper headlines about reports of scandals that have occurred within the Church in the past few decades—particularly incidences that have involved young people. Yes, some unfortunate individuals have betrayed their vocations and committed heinous crimes. Innocent people have been victimized and traumatized as a result of it, which no amount of money can rectify. As Christians, we need to pray for both the violated and those that have offended. But we also have to keep in mind that a minute group of individuals who have been found guilty of such crimes in no way implies that all priests and religious are untrustworthy and inclined to commit such acts. The fact is that over 99% of the men and women who serve God in a religious vocation are good and holy people who have made tremendous sacrifices in order to follow God's call. They deserve our compassion and respect. The Church is working hard to ensure that these events do not happen again, but in the meantime, the situation has made the vocation of good religious even harder, and for that they need our prayers more than ever.

It's important to realize as Catholics that we cannot rely solely on mainstream media for accurate reporting on matters involving the Catholic Church. We must supplement our knowledge with reputable Catholic news sources. The truth is that inappropriate behavior involving young people has occurred to an even greater degree in public schools and in other religious denominations. The reason the Catholic Church makes the news is because we profess high standards that the rest of the world doesn't want to hear. Many people and groups are bent on proving that priestly celibacy is a failed model, and they use these new stories to defend their argument. Since priests are the representation of Christ on earth and the ones who bring Jesus to their flocks through the sacraments, they will always be persecuted, just as Jesus himself was persecuted. That will never change until the end of time.

The good in all of this is that these terrible incidents needed to come to the light so that we as a Church can take responsibility for them, prevent them from happening in the future, and move on, stronger and wiser and better equipped to proclaim the Gospel to the world.

Spiritually Adopting a Seminarian

One of the ways our family has come to have a deeper appreciation for the Sacrament of Holy Orders is by "spiritually adopting" a seminarian.

The Journey to Priesthood

We had the good fortune of getting to know a man named Steve from our parish who was discerning a religious vocation. Steve had been adopted and raised in the Baptist faith, but by his teen years, he began a spiritual journey in which he dabbled in many faiths including Anabaptist, Jehovah's Witness, Mormon, Presbyterian, and a handful of others before he found his way to the Catholic Church. Soon after, Steve discerned a calling to the priesthood. His parents were not thrilled when Steve decided to convert to Catholicism, but his decision to pursue the priesthood was really too much for them. Emotionally, they were unable to be a part of his religious pursuits, and that's when our family stepped in. We saw this as a perfect opportunity to expose our boys to the journey to priesthood (and to learn a few things ourselves in the process). We spiritually adopted Steve and proudly attended the milestones along the way, such as when he received the ministries of Lector, Acolyte, and Deacon. We bought him his first clericals and a Mass Kit and truly felt like an important part of his religious formation.

I recall with particular fondness the day that Steve received the ministries of Lector and Acolyte. The beautiful liturgy was followed by a brunch for family and friends served in the dining hall of the seminary. Our boys were much younger then, and as was our custom, they were all dressed exactly alike in their striped shirts. Needless to say, we were quite an entourage. Just as we were beginning to enjoy our breakfast, the bishop who had presided over the liturgy walked into the dining hall and caught sight of our four boys. He came right over to our table and gave them a big, beaming smile. "Well," he chortled, "tell me. Which one of you is going to become a priest?"

My breath caught in my throat. This was the moment I had waited for all my life. It was the question I had asked myself a million times. I sat up erect to hear which youngster would be inspired by the Holy Spirit to answer this proverbial question. Our third son, Daniel, who was five years old at the time, piped up. "Well," he said, in answer to the bishop's question, "that would be... my mom." For a split second there was silence at this unexpected answer. Then the bishop let out a roaring laugh that set the whole dining room to laughter. Meanwhile, I was sinking slowly into my chair, shocked and embarrassed by my son's response. That was *not* the answer I was hoping to hear.

As I thought about it, however, I realized why Daniel had given the bishop that answer. He and his brothers were quite accustomed to me constantly saying things like, "Wouldn't it be cool to be a priest? Wouldn't it be amazing to hold the host in your hands and have it turn to *Jesus*? Wouldn't it be awesome to hear people's confessions and help them with their problems?" Of course, I was making these comments with the intention of planting seeds in their little minds about the idea that one of them might become a priest one day. Evidently, Daniel had missed this intention and was thinking all along that *I* wanted to be a priest. Suffice it to say, I had a little conversation with him as we ate our eggs about why Mommy wasn't being called to the priesthood. But secretly I was delighted in the fact that my son had gotten the message, skewed as it was, that religious life is a calling to be honored in others and prayerfully considered for oneself.

Nuns in Nashville

Our friends have a daughter who is now a fully professed Dominican Sister of the Congregation of St. Cecilia in Nashville, Tennessee. In striking contrast to many religious orders in the U.S. that are decreasing in size and increasing in age, the "Nashville Dominicans," as they are known, are bursting at the seams with over 250 members, the average age of which is 36. They are an energetic, enthusiastic, and traditional community with a deep love for the Lord and the Church, and many of them are being prepared to serve in education, which is a blessing for our future generations. I often fantasize about what it would be like to have a

Nashville Dominican at the helm of every parochial school
in the country.

Sister Kateri Rose, our friends' daughter, is one of the
bubbliest people I've ever met, and discovering her religious
calling has only magnified this. Our family spiritually
adopted her when she first entered the order. Her seven
years of formation was for the most part cloistered, so we
did not get to see her often in person. But we stayed in
touch through letters and Christmas cards, and prayed for
her continually. Her picture hung on our refrigerator, and
the boys were happy to know a real religious sister in the
making. The day we attended her first profession of vows,
we met another young sister who had even a bigger smile
than Kateri's. When we learned that this girl's parents were
atheists and not supportive at that time of their daughter's
discernment to a religious life, we spiritually adopted her
as well.

I tell you about Steve and Kateri in the hopes that
it will inspire you to think about spiritually adopting a
seminarian, religious novice, or retired priest, sister, or
brother. It's a great activity for families and for students in
the classroom and a wonderful way to make the vocation of
religious life come alive for children. The relationship will
vary according to situation. It may consist of letter writing,
picture drawing, care packages or personal visits, but always
first and foremost—prayer! It can also vary according to
the age and situation of the person you adopt. We've had
the pleasure of visiting a retired sister at a local Dominican
motherhouse several times in the past, and the sisters would
always light up when the boys came with us. Retirement can

be very isolating for a religious, and a visit (especially one with children) can really lift spirits.

Behind the Walls

The last group of people I want to mention in this chapter is one that tends to be forgotten in our busy world today—cloistered religious, men and women who live their lives of faith, work, and prayer behind convent and monastery walls. These communities should never be taken for granted, because it is the constant prayer, sacrifice, and Eucharistic Adoration of these holy men and women that keeps this world spinning on its axis. Wise religious leaders and organizations throughout history have recognized the critical importance of a religious community in providing prayerful support for the success of their missions. Every five years, for example, a new group of cloistered nuns moves into the Vatican for the express purpose of praying for the pontiff. In a similar manner, anyone who is affiliated with the largest religious media in the world, Mother Angelica's Eternal World Television Network (EWTN), will confirm that the enormous success of the station's radio and television broadcasting efforts is attributed to the constant prayers of Mother's religious community.

In my hometown of Columbus, Ohio, we have the great privilege to be within driving distance of the Abbey at Gethsemani, the Trappist monastery best known as the home of the late Catholic monk and author, Thomas Merton. A few years ago, I slipped away from my boisterous and busy household for a few days of silence and solitude among another family of men, the Trappist monks. Although a cloistered order, The Trappists see visitors as a sign of Christ, and they welcome them warmly as guests in their retreat house. Pilgrims are invited to join the monks as they gather to pray seven times each day during all hours of the day and night. It's hard not to be profoundly touched by these special disciples who are committed to maintaining this ancient tradition of prayer and monastic life.

I learned a great deal observing the life of these monks. To an outside observer, the apparent limitations and monotony of monastic life can seem harsh and undesirable. Some might accuse the monk of running away from reality or wasting his time in such an obscure existence. But I came to realize that the kind of person who comes to a monastery and stays is a person running not *from* something but *to* something. In terms of exterior things, he has finished his search and is ready to begin a new interior search. This does not mean that he's exempt from the challenges of sin, disillusionment, or distraction that all of us face in our own lives. Rather, he has simply found his home and his vocation. When I thought about this, I realized that the monk is not all that different from me. As I live out God's plan as a married person with children, I too am faced with limitations, structure, and responsibilities. In the end, though, I have discovered that these confinements are actually liberating and necessary for my spiritual growth and are what will ultimately lead me to true joy and fulfillment.

By the third day of my retreat at Gethsemani, as I was finally acclimating to the routine of monastic life, I found myself beginning to miss my family and my schedule. As blissful as this place of prayer was, I was still an outsider there, among strangers, and it made me feel somewhat lonely. I realized I hadn't really escaped routine—I had merely adopted another. Gazing at the picture of the boys I had stuck between the pages of my journal, I found I missed their little faces. I missed their *noise*. One of the last things I did before leaving my retreat was to sit in the choir loft overlooking the empty monastery church. I gazed down at the opposing choir stalls below where the monks would convene to pray and considered how they were no longer filled to capacity as they were in the days of Thomas Merton. The thought of half-empty choir stalls challenged me to look at my own life and wonder how I was limited in my own spirituality. Was I only a shadow of my potential, of what God has planned for me? What did I need to do to make my "house of prayer" more vibrant and alive? I packed my bags, pondering that reflection.

Then I returned to the world to which God has called me: a world of soccer cleats, bug jars, laundry, dishes, and unfinished manuscripts—and all the subsequent noise that comes with it. I think often about the monks at the Abbey of Gethsemani. They have taught me a great deal about the value of finding quiet time in my own busy day to praise God. When I look at the clock, I remember when the monks are in prayer, at work, or asleep. I pray for these special men and their gift to the world. And I petition for those choir stalls to be filled once again to capacity, echoing with the sound of young voices singing the eternal verses: "*Praise the Father, Son, and the Holy Spirit. Both now and forever. The God who is, who was, and is to come at the end of the ages…*"

Connecting Home and Monastery

I am a big advocate of going on retreat to recharge the batteries and get a fresh perspective on life. Granted, it means precious time away from the family, but an occasional retreat can do wonders for ourselves and our loved ones. There are other ways, too, that our families can experience the beauty of monastic life. Is there a convent or monastery near your home that you can tell your children about, or even better, visit together? Perhaps it is possible to exchange letters with one of the monks or nuns who lives there. Learn as a family about the various monastic orders in our country and abroad, and remember to keep these communities close to your heart in prayer. They are certainly praying for us!

Looking Ahead...

All followers of Christ are called to serve, but some are called to a distinctive life of service through the role of priest, deacon, religious sister or brother. God calls whom he wills to this life, and it is our job as parents to create an openness in the hearts and minds of our children to respond if this is their vocation. For this is where they will find true joy. A good way to do this is by befriending those with religious vocations in our parishes, schools, and communities. In this chapter, we talked about spiritually adopting seminarians and religious who are in formation. We also remember priests and religious who reside in cloisters as well as those living their final years in retirement centers, nursing homes, and hospitals. In the next chapter, we will give more consideration to the elderly and infirm as we discuss our final sacrament, the Anointing of the Sick.

7

STRENGTH FOR THE SUFFERING

The Sacrament of the Anointing of the Sick

In Scripture, Jesus is portrayed time and time again as the divine healer. He could heal people through his word alone, as in the case of the centurion's servant. We also read of the woman with a hemorrhage, too frightened to ask for a healing, who drew power out of Jesus simply by touching the hem of his garment. In most of his healings, however, Jesus deliberately touched those who were sick with his hands. Wherever he went, people gathered in great numbers, bringing their ailing loved ones to the One who could make the blind see, the lame walk, the possessed free, and the dead come to life again. These miraculous wonders gave witness to the fact that Jesus was "the One who is to come" as prophesized by John the Baptist. Indeed, the Kingdom of God was at hand.

But Jesus could do more than heal the physical body. He could also heal the *soul*, and he exercised this God-given power through the forgiveness of sins, much to the consternation of the Jewish leaders of his day. Furthermore, he endowed his Apostles with similar healing abilities, and they went out and laid hands on the people, anointed them with oil, and prayed for their healing in the name of Jesus.

Jesus' evident love for the sick and suffering sets forth a powerful commission to us as Christian followers that we, too, are called to care for those who are ill, less fortunate, or otherwise on the margins of society. In Charles Dickens' classic, *A Christmas Carol*, the cold-hearted and greedy moneylender, Ebenezer Scrooge, is given a rare second chance to learn a powerful lesson. His accounting partner returns from the grave to admonish Ebenezer that as far as heaven is concerned, Ebenezer's business is *mankind*, not the miserly livelihood on the stock exchange that has come to obsess him. As the story goes, Ebenezer sees the error of his ways and becomes a kind and generous man. Dickens is presenting a moral lesson for all of us. We will not be asked in heaven about the size of our house, the awards we won, or the car we drove. We will be asked instead how we remembered the widowed, the orphaned, the imprisoned, and the infirm. How were we the eyes, arms, voice, and heart of Jesus on earth to those we encountered, particularly the suffering?

A Sacrament for the Sick and Suffering

No healthy-minded person *likes* to suffer. But suffering brings with it opportunities for great gifts and graces. Whether our pain is physical, spiritual or emotional, there is power and blessing in it when we can unite our torments and afflictions with the suffering of Christ. As I explain to young people, when we join our pain and hardships with Jesus, the One who suffered more than anyone on earth ever has or ever will, a true miracle happens. There is a mystical explosion of grace that showers down not only on us, but on others who really need it—others we may never even know. Suffering often provides the impetus for us to turn to God and recognize our dependence on him. It enables us to develop the important virtues of humility, patience, and fortitude and helps us to deepen our faith and trust in God. A natural part of suffering, especially long-term suffering, is the temptation to despair. In our physical and emotional anguish, we can grow weak in our faith and ask God why he hasn't answered our prayers for healing and relief. The Sacrament of the Anointing of the Sick can help us find meaning in our pain and suffering and give us consolation for our journey.

The Anointing of the Sick is a sacrament that can only be conferred by a priest or bishop. The one who is afflicted is anointed on the forehead and hands with oil that has been blessed by the bishop at a Chrism Mass during Holy Week. In the early Church, the anointing was meant for anyone who was sick or suffering in some way. Over the centuries, however, the sacrament was delegated for those who were nearing death and became known as "Extreme Unction." As you can imagine, people developed a fear about this sacrament, since it indicated death was imminent. You can also imagine how many people died before the priest arrived to anoint them. Vatican II helped to restore the original name of the sacrament, the Anointing of the Sick, as well as its original function. No longer is the sacrament reserved for those at the point of death. Today it is commonly administered to those battling serious illness and those about to undergo surgery, as well as those who are in danger of death due to advancing age or medical conditions. People suffering from chronic mental illnesses, such as addiction and depression, are also encouraged to receive an anointing.

Many people think of the Anointing of the Sick as a private affair that is administered by a priest in the home or the hospital. While it can be administered this way, there is a growing trend to celebrate this sacrament as a community (as all sacraments are meant be celebrated) in the form of a healing Mass. Whether administered publicly or privately, the Anointing of the Sick, through the grace of the Holy Spirit, confers strength, peace, and courage to help people contend with serious illnesses or advanced age. It helps people renew their trust and faith in God and overcome the temptation to give in to despair. The sacrament also helps a person unite his or her suffering to Christ and offers with it the forgiveness of sin to complete the healing. In some cases, the Anointing of the Sick can serve as preparation for the final journey of life and is most efficacious when accompanied by *Viaticum*, the final reception of the Eucharist. These powerful end-of-life sacraments assure the dying that they are not alone in their darkest hour: Jesus is walking with them through this mystery.

What Children Can Learn about the Anointing of the Sick

You might consider it rather unusual to be discussing the Anointing of the Sick with your young children. Hopefully, they will not need this sacrament themselves for a very long time. But illness and death are a natural part of life, and sheltering our children from that reality only delays their acceptance of it. The philosophy of my husband

and me has been to expose our children to the reality of illness and death by looking for opportunities to take them on visits to hospitals, nursing homes, or funeral parlors, particularly when the person we are visiting is someone other than immediate family. In this way, our children are more prepared when the person who needs our prayers is someone closer to home.

Full Cycle of Sacramental Life

I remember taking our oldest son, Michael, when he was about four years old, to a Mass at a nearby parish one morning. It happened to be a funeral Mass, so I sat in the back with him, quietly explaining what was happening. The funeral was for a 99-year-old great-grandmother whose family showed more smiles of joy for a life well-lived than tears of grief. I was proud of how well I was handling this unexpected teaching moment, until the two of us went up for Communion and walked past the casket stationed in the center aisle. Michael looked up at me and said nonchalantly and a bit too loudly, "Who's in the box?" I hurried him out the door and continued our lesson on the drive home.

Taking children to a Catholic Funeral Mass (barring any awkward moments) is a wonderful opportunity to teach young ones about the full cycle of sacramental life. Through this special liturgy, we as Catholics proclaim our faith in Jesus' victory over death and our hope in resurrection. We believe that death is not the end, but the beginning of a perfect and permanent life with Christ in heaven. Therefore, it is truly a celebration, even though we experience a temporary separation from one we love. Use the moment to point out to your children how the white cloth or *pall* that covers the casket at the funeral is similar to the white garment an infant or small child wears during baptism. It symbolizes that we are washed clean of our sins by the blood of the Lamb, that we have put on Christ, and that we are a new creation in him. The white represents purity and truth and serves as an outward sign of our belief in our Christian dignity that we work hard to bring unstained into eternal life. Show children how the Easter or Paschal candle is present at the final liturgical celebration of a Catholic's life, as it is in their first sacrament of baptism. It burns brightly to symbolize the light of the Risen Christ and our belief that he has conquered the darkness of sin and death. As the priest blesses the casket with holy water, we can remind our children of the waters of baptism that made us sons and daughters of God and filled us with the Holy Spirit. In baptism we died and rose again with Christ; this destiny is our prayerful hope for the one whose funeral we celebrate.

Life Lessons Affiliated with This Sacrament

Because the Sacrament of the Anointing of the Sick is one that most reminds us of our mortality, it can easily be tied to a number of important life lessons we can impart to our children regarding spiritual living, dying, and the eternal life to come.

Sanctity of Life

First, it's important to discuss with children the sanctity of human life in all its various stages from natural conception to natural death. According to their age and understanding, we can speak with children about the sacredness and gift of life, how it begins, and God's intention for the miracle of new life to take place within the marriage of a loving husband and wife. Long before our children will become sexually active, it's a good idea to make it a point to discuss things like contraception and in vitro fertilization and how these practices conflict with the natural order and God's careful design.

Respect for Those Who Are Different

While each of us is endowed with unique gifts and abilities, all people have an equal dignity in the eyes of God. We can convey this message to our children by instilling in them a respect for people who look or sound different than we do (in particular, for people with disabilities), talking to them about the damaging effects of hurtful remarks and stares. It's a good practice to thank God for the abilities he has given us. One of the ways my husband and I have tried to help make our children more appreciative of the marvelous bodies they have received from God is to include in our nighttime prayers a litany of gratefulness for how we were made: "Thank you God for eyes to see, ears to hear, nose to smell, mouth to speak, hands to touch, feet to walk, brain to think, heart to love, and a strong, healthy body!"

Our Body as a Temple of God

Another way we can show appreciation for the gift of life we have received from God is to have a healthy respect for our bodies. Good hygiene, modest attire, proper diet, and exercise are important messages young people need to hear today. Equally important is the message to honor and respect the bodies of others. When children are young, this can be translated into keeping our hands to ourselves. For older children, respecting the bodies of others, particular those of the opposite sex, means using respectful words and actions in their presence and avoiding the lure of pornography.

Putting the Works of Mercy to Work

The beautiful Catholic tradition of the Corporal Works of Mercy is a powerful aid to family unity and spiritual growth, as they help us to love and serve others as Jesus asked. At Lent, our family posts the Corporal Works of Mercy in our kitchen, checking each one off as we fulfill them during the weeks leading to Easter. In addition to helping those who are hungry, thirsty, naked, homeless, or imprisoned, the Corporal Works of Mercy encourage us to visit the sick and bury the dead. Children can bring a special light to those who are lonely and suffering, particularly those who are advanced in age. We've taken our sons to nursing homes, retirement villages, and hospitals to perform music, drop off a picture, or just bring a smile. Such interactions help develop in our children a respectful attitude for the aging and infirm. With the current trend of multi-generational families sharing the same home, children are once again reaping the benefits of spending time with older relatives who can offer a great deal of life experience. While moments of stress and compromise are a natural part of that living arrangement, the overall benefit of a grandparent-grandchild relationship yields tremendous fruit.

One of the other Corporal Works of Mercy my husband and I do with our boys is remembering the imprisoned. In addition to sending books and other spiritual literature to local correctional facilities, our family corresponds with an incarcerated man in Florida who was sentenced to death row over thirty years ago for a crime that modern science proves he never committed. Since Florida law does not recognize the admission of new evidence after a certain period of time, this man continues to remain imprisoned unjustly, never knowing whether tomorrow will be his last day. Remarkably, he has not lost his spirit. He is a deeply trusting man whose faith in God is an example and a challenge to our entire family.

In addition to the Corporal Works of Mercy, there are Spiritual Works of Mercy. These include instructing the ignorant, counseling the doubtful, admonishing sinners, bearing wrongs patiently, forgiving offenses willingly, comforting the afflicted, and praying for the living and the dead. Look for opportunities in your family to exercise these important works as well.

Talking about Eternity in the Here and Now

The Anointing of the Sick gives us the perfect opening to speak with our children about the reality of heaven, hell, and purgatory. While we may not hear these realities preached about as much from Catholic pulpits today, the fact is we each have an eternal destiny awaiting us that only we can determine. Many parents spend time with their children establishing goals and plans for the future, which is important and motivational, but how many of us consider our goals and plans for what comes *after* this life? The way we live our lives on this earth paves the road for our final destination. As Catholics, our goal is to get to heaven and bring with us as many people as we can. We are only pilgrims traveling through this life, and our existence here is short compared to eternity. We want to make sure we are choosing the *right* eternity. The world today tends to downplay the concept of hell and the devil, which is logical, because the prince of darkness is strong and operates best when people ignore his existence. But hell is an absolute reality. Some of the most powerful descriptions of hell I've ever read come from the visions of Sister Josefa Menendez in her book *Way of Divine Love*. She was mystically transported to hell several times to witness to the rest of us the great suffering that occurs there. As far as purgatory is concerned, Susan Tassone has authored books on the importance of praying for the departed souls who can no longer pray for themselves. These provide an excellent introduction to the concept of purgatory and are a good source of encouragement for making these poor souls a focus of our family prayer. Our family also enjoys praying the prayer of St. Gertrude, which tradition says releases one thousand souls from purgatory every time it is recited:

> "Eternal Father, I offer Thee the Most Precious Blood of Thy Divine Son, Jesus, in union with the Masses said throughout the world today, for all the holy souls in Purgatory, for sinners everywhere, for sinners in the universal church, those in my own home and within my family. Amen."

Whether or not the number of souls said to be released with that prayer is accurate, our family takes comfort knowing that our prayers are serving others, and that we are performing this important Spiritual Work of Mercy.

Fostering a Regard for Life

The Anointing of the Sick is a sacrament designed to celebrate and support life in its most difficult moments. This is critical, because we live in a culture in which the sacredness of life is being threatened by economic and political agendas. As our nation's government leaders struggle to address the burgeoning cost of health care by creating a policy of sweeping reform, I, like many people, worry about who will benefit and who will lose from such a system. Certainly there is a valid concern for the unborn and the potential of abortion to increase in the future through the help of federal funding. But I also worry about the elderly. Will grandma be considered too old and not worth the investment of an expensive surgery that may not be successful anyway? And what about those with disabilities? Will they be allowed to receive health care procedures when they desperately need them? Will they even be allowed to be born in the first place? Will government makes these decisions? Will families? And regardless of who makes the decisions, will people decide that the sick are too great a financial burden? In a culture that is not committed to defending the dignity of life in all its forms, I'm afraid that if people are given the choice of holding onto their money or paying for health care for the marginalized, they are more likely to choose the money.

These thoughts are chilling to me. The wisdom of people such as the Blessed Teresa of Calcutta and Pope John Paul II tell us that the measure of a civilization is how it treats its weakest members. If that's the case, our country may one day have some serious accounting to do before the Lord of Life. In violating the Gospel message of taking care of the least of his people, we are not helping to usher in the Kingdom of God, but rather, we open the door to usher in God's wrath. Of course, our country is not the only one guilty of such disregard for life. For years, many European nations have been leading the way in legalizing procedures such as abortion and euthanasia. One hamlet of hope in Europe, however, proclaims a powerful message of elevating the dignity of humanity, one that stands in stark contrast to the rest of the continent. I'm referring to the little town of Lourdes, France, the site of the world-famous apparitions of the Virgin Mary to St. Bernadette Soubirous in 1858 and one of the largest centers of physical, spiritual, and emotional healing in the world today.

The Miracle of Lourdes

I had the good fortune to be sent to Lourdes in 2005 to write a book commemorating the 150th anniversary of the apparitions, *Lourdes: Font of Faith, Hope, and Charity.* I had never been to Lourdes before, so I went with my husband with the intention of experiencing the place as a pilgrim first, and an investigative journalist second. During my pilgrimage, I was able to interview the bishop, the medical director, the rector, the director of hospitality, and several chaplains and volunteers, to get an insider's perspective of the shrine. What was most striking to me was the powerful demonstration of compassion and respect for those with illness and disabilities that seemed to permeate the shrine. My husband has worked for more than twenty years accommodating people with disabilities in their homes and at their places of work, and he was particularly taken by the intricate ramping systems that run throughout the hilly shrine to enable every wheelchair and gurney to reach its intended destinations.

Lourdes is a place that welcomes all people, despite their faith (or lack thereof), their social status, or their present health condition. But it is those who suffer from serious physical and mental illnesses that are the privileged guests and VIPs of the sanctuary. These are the people who are given the front rows of the Masses and the first positions in the processionals. It is they who inspire thousands of volunteers from around the world—many of them teenagers—to spend their personal money and vacation time to come to Lourdes and serve. You see these cheerful volunteers assisting in the bath, making beds in the *accueil* (a cross between a hotel and a hospital), serving food in the cafeteria, or performing crowd control during the procession. The volunteers are trained not only in their particular services, but in the spirit of Bernadette—that is, to care for the suffering with tenderness and love. In Lourdes, pilgrims are invited to live out the two greatest commandments: to love God and to love one another.

Miracles are an everyday occurrence at Lourdes. Sometimes they are the powerful medical miracles that are studied and documented by the Medical Bureau. But the great majority of miracles for the six million pilgrims who come to the sanctuary each year are the interior ones: a conversion of heart; the peaceful acceptance of one's cross; a recognition that we are not alone in our suffering and brokenness; the courage to live our lives more fully; and a deepened love for God. My experience in Lourdes reminded me that suffering is not always indicated by a wheelchair or some other outward sign—often, suffering can be deep and hidden from the outside world. I also returned from Lourdes more aware of those suffering in my own family and community and how important it is that these beloved of God are treated with mercy and understanding. This to me is one of the greatest miracles of Lourdes.

Walking the Final Journey

As lay people, we are not able to administer the Sacrament of the Anointing of the Sick, but we *are* encouraged to lay hands on those who suffer, read Scripture with them, bring them Jesus in the Eucharist, and pray for a healing of body and soul. In some cases, we are asked to accompany individuals on their final journey of life.

This was to be the case involving a dear friend of ours, Caroline, to whom this book is dedicated. My husband and I had met Caroline and her husband through Marriage Encounter. This energetic couple exhibited a playful passion for one another that was contagious and made us want to be around them. Caroline was a powerful presence with a fervent love for her Catholic faith, an intense dedication to her husband and the six children she homeschooled, a zeal for life, and an uncanny knack for making the person she was with feel like the most important person in the world. Everywhere this woman went she exuded joy and enthusiasm. Her twinkling eyes, quick smile, and boisterous laugh would light up the room, and I was drawn to her immediately. We would meet monthly for lunch to swap notes about marriage, parenting, life, and our dreams as Catholic writers. Just as I was thinking this vibrant woman was the most perfect friend I could ever have, we received devastating news: Caroline had fourth stage lung cancer.

Now, Caroline was a fighter, having successfully battled cervical cancer ten years prior. She had in her favor her relative youth and the fact that she was a non-smoker and otherwise in good health, but still the doctors were clear about the dismal survival rates from such an advanced disease. Caroline and her husband had an unwavering faith in God and the support of an enormous community of people that they had touched over the years, and they were ready for battle. My friend turned to me for hope, and that's where I focused my energy and efforts. We prayed together and talked about life. We explored dietary options to slow the growth of the cancer, and I took her to a master herbalist for supplements. We pilgrimaged to St. Anthony's Chapel in Pittsburgh that houses over 4,000 relics (the largest collection outside of the Vatican). There, a sister prayed over Caroline with a relic of the True Cross. I even took her to a powerful healing priest who prayed over my sick friend and anointed her. Caroline would actually receive the Anointing of the Sick several times, which gave her great peace of mind.

Despite Caroline's resolution to get well, her health continued to decline. As the cancer spread and her medications were increased, I began to realize that my efforts had not achieved the results we had hoped for, and I felt helpless and upset that God would allow this to happen. Eventually, medical intervention was ceased and Hospice was called in, but still Caroline clung to the hope that a miracle was possible, even now. In a last-ditch effort, my husband and I and several members of her support group sent Caroline and her husband to Lourdes. Our thought was that even if a physical cure was not God's plan, the couple might discover the strength and peace to finish this difficult journey. Their pilgrimage to Lourdes was beautiful, but even two immersions in the waters of the spring did not deter the cancer that continued to ravage Caroline's body. Two weeks after their return, she died at home with her husband at her side, the way she had wanted it.

Caroline had lost the battle against cancer. But she claimed a victory that was far more important. Through her repeated anointing and daily reception of Holy Eucharist, Caroline was empowered by the sacraments to stay close to Jesus throughout her journey. She never lost hope or faith. As St. Paul says, she had fought the good fight and won, and her example allowed her family to remain faithful as well.

Even with the passage of time, I miss my friend terribly. I miss our lunches and our ambitious plans for how we were going to change the world through our writing. I still don't understand the plan of God to take a woman in the prime of her life from a family who loved her—a woman with so much promise and conviction to do God's work on earth. I can only surmise it's because she is needed to do his work in a greater capacity in heaven. She's still a prayer warrior, fighting the good fight; she's just serving on a different place in the battlefield.

I took our boys with me on one of my last visits to see Caroline so they could let her know they were praying for her and could give some form of comfort to her own children, whom they had befriended as easily as we had befriended the parents. I know this wasn't easy for them, because it's every child's greatest fear to lose a parent. But I'm glad we made this visit as a family, because our boys continue to pray for their friends (and for the soul of Caroline) without any prompting from us. They entered into this difficult situation, physically and emotionally, calling upon their faith to make sense of it all.

Caroline's life—and death—taught our family poignant lessons. The first lesson we learned is what it means to live fully and to die faithfully. We saw the power of faith and the sacraments at work in this family in the form of strength, nurturing, healing, and courage, and we have complete confidence that Caroline left this world fortified by God's abundant grace. Second, we learned that sometimes people are allowed to suffer so that others may come forth in love and compassion. We saw this demonstrated in an endless stream of visitors, food preparers, errand runners, and housecleaners—and even more so, in the outpouring of emotion, affection, and witnessing at the funeral home. Third, we learned that despite our hopes for a miracle, sometimes death is the ultimate physical healing. Fourth, we learned how something like this could happen to any family—even ours—and how important it is, therefore, to cherish every day of life we are given.

I tell my boys that when we as faithful Christians are faced with a life-threatening illness, there are two doors set before us. Jesus is standing between the two doors. One door represents a cure and a return to health, which simply means that God has more work for us to do on earth. The other door indicates our heavenly reward. The important thing is that Jesus stands at both doors, ready to accompany us through the one that God desires. We are never alone, nor are the loved ones we may be asked to leave behind for a time. This thought is most comforting to me. As a Catholic, I am eternally grateful for the unique gift of the Anointing of the Sick and the blessing this sacrament offers in our time of greatest need.

Looking Ahead...

Jesus, the Divine Healer, left us with the Sacrament of the Anointing of the Sick to extend his physical and spiritual healing presence to those who suffer. This sacrament brings peace and strength, especially at those times we are tempted to despair. While we cannot administer this sacrament as lay people, we can certainly be a healing presence to others through our prayers and charitable works of mercy. We can also use the sacrament to teach our children important lessons about the sanctity and dignity of life in all its various stages. In learning about the Sacrament of the Anointing of the Sick, we have rounded out our discussion of the seven sacraments. Where to go from here? That will be the subject of our final chapter.

CONCLUSION

Taking the First Step

I hope this book has given you some thought starters on ways you can incorporate the seven sacraments more integrally into your family for more joyous Catholic living. There are a lot of suggestions in this book. Share them with your family and begin implementing the ones that make the most sense to you. Brainstorm your own ideas and traditions. The most important thing is to look for ways to harness the sacraments to bring healing, nourishment, strength, and protection into your family experience. And don't underestimate the significance of this. When we revitalize the family through God's graces, we revitalize the Church and, in turn, the world!

The Domestic Church

In ancient Christian times, the family was considered a domestic church. Each family was the center of a living and radiant faith in an unbelieving world and represented the first schools of Christian life and virtue, especially when nurtured by prayer, the sacraments, acts of charity and service, and joyful living. The Second Vatican Council resurrected the term "domestic church," recognizing the dignity and holiness of family life. In its document, *Lumen*

Gentium, it called upon modern Catholic families to see their value for education and evangelization in a rapidly secularized world. Specifically, it called upon parents, the heart of the domestic church, bonded in the Sacrament of Marriage, to serve as the first preachers of the faith for their children by word and example. Today, we need the powerful witness of family more than ever.

Sacramental Living

An authentic Catholic family is called to live a sacramental life. By that I mean we are called to understand, prepare, and participate in the sacraments instituted by Jesus, which are necessary for our salvation. We've already seen the powerful ways these sacraments can assist us at every stage of human development. However, we are also invited to further nurture and protect our families through the use of *sacramentals,* objects and actions given to us by the Church to help us live a life of prayer and to celebrate the feasts of the liturgical year. They can be material objects like the rosary, the scapular, the Advent Wreath, the Miraculous Medal, holy water, statues, or crucifixes. Or they can be actions such as the Sign of the Cross, genuflection, hands extended in prayer, or the washing of feet on Holy Thursday. While sacraments give us direct grace, *sacramentals* afford us an indirect grace that is also valuable to the well-being of our families. These indirect graces include forgiveness of venial sins, remission of temporal punishment of sins (i.e., rectifying the lingering negative effects of our sinful actions), health of body and material blessings, and protection from evil spirits. Today, our families can use all the grace we can get!

In living a sacramental life, the Catholic family home—
the domestic church—becomes consecrated ground. It
blossoms into a visible reminder of our faith and our love
for God, not just to the family members, but to all who visit
our homes. As an example of this, some years ago, our family
learned about the tradition of enthroning the home to the
Sacred Heart of Jesus. We liked the idea of declaring Jesus
Christ the King of our household and the true head of our
family. After doing some research, we put together a small
ceremony and invited friends and family to attend. Our
deacon graciously agreed to preside over the celebration. Our
"enthroned" picture of Jesus, with his Sacred Heart exposed,
hangs near the front door of our home to welcome visitors,
and it is where our family gathers on our knees when we are
practicing family prayer.

In addition to our Enthroned Sacred Heart, we keep
holy water fonts at our front and back doors, which
admittedly are hard to keep filled due to evaporation,
but we like the idea of blessing ourselves as we leave and
enter our home. My husband and I also make it a habit of
blessing our children at night or when they leave for school.
We have blessed crucifixes hanging above the doorways of
every bedroom, and we've had a priest bless our home. We
perpetuate this blessing by sprinkling the rooms with holy
water routinely as a family and even blessing the perimeters
of our yard with holy salt. At Christmas time, our home
is decorated to celebrate the Incarnation and at Easter to
celebrate Jesus' resurrection. During Lent our home is
adorned with purple flowers and accents. Changing the
decorations to match the liturgical year helps us to remain
connected to Mother Church. Most precious to us are the

times we've had Mass celebrated in our home by a dear priest friend when he visits.

A Final Reflection

As we think back over what we've learned about the seven sacraments, from Holy Baptism to the Anointing of the Sick, we realize that as Catholics, we are born in God, we live in God, and we die in God. The seven sacraments are like a mysterious and beautiful thread that weaves through the experience of Catholic life. We know that God's love, like God himself, is eternal. He has *always* loved us, even before we were capable of existing. The sacraments are a way for us to respond to that love and celebrate what God has done for us in our past and our present, and what he promises to do in our future. Jesus gave us the sacraments so we can always remain connected to him. They help us to grow in faith and become better followers of Christ. I like to tell young people that the seven sacraments are like seven hugs from Jesus.

So where do we go from here? Every journey begins with the first step. To most effectively teach the faith to our children and inspire within them a deeper appreciation of the sacraments, we need to begin with an honest look at our own spirituality. As parents, grandparents, godparents, teachers, and catechists, we need to ask ourselves important questions: Are we on fire about our Catholic faith? Do we participate in the sacraments regularly and worthily? Are we seeking change in ourselves and growth in our relationship with God through the sacraments? Are the sacraments alive for us—are they true encounters with Jesus Christ?

If we cannot answer these questions with a resounding "yes!" this is the place we can begin. When we understand, appreciate, and embrace the sacraments, they will truly transform us. Then our love and enthusiasm, no longer able to be contained, will brim over and we will be well equipped to hand on the tremendous treasure of our Catholic faith to our children and all those we encounter in love.

May God bless you always!

ENDNOTES

1 An earlier version of this material was first published in *America*, May 6, 2002.

2 "Confessions of a Catholic Convert," *St. Anthony Messenger*, 2003.

3 These miracles are the subject of my recent book, *Bleeding Hands, Weeping Stone: True Stories of Divine Wonders, Miracles, and Messages* (St. Benedict Press / TAN Books).

4 As it turned out, St. Thérèse was not only the subject of my first published article, which marked the beginning of my ministry in Catholic writing, but the subject of my first adult book as well. See *Shower of Heavenly Roses: Stories of the Intercession of St. Thérèse of Lisieux* (The Crossroad Publishing Company).

OF RELATED INTEREST

Keith Frome, Ed.D.

HOW'S MY KID DOING?

Practical Answers to Questions about Your Child's Education

Foreword Magazine Medal Winner!

"Frome combines two decades of concrete experience with a warmth and wisdom that help you understand your kid, your school, and yourself more clearly than ever."

—Kinney Zalesne, coauthor, *Microtrends: The Small Forces Behind Tomorrow's Big Changes*

While children are known for asking tough questions wherever they go, their parents often feel left alone with the overwhelming challenges of education in today's complex world. Longtime headmaster and educator Keith Frome has listened to parents for years. In this helpful book he gathers sound, practical advice on a multitude of parents' most pressing questions along with the latest research and trends regarding homework, curriculum, discipline, and social and moral issues. A rare and valuable resource for every parent of a child K-12.

978-0-8245-2424-1, paperback

OF RELATED INTEREST

David Robinson
THE BUSY FAMILY'S GUIDE TO SPIRITUALITY
Practical Lessons for Modern Living from the Monastic Tradition

"The most innovative book I have seen in family spirituality."

—Spiritual Life

Drawing on timeless principles of monastic communal living, this spiritual guide for families offers effective tools to meet today's challenges and counteract the divisive forces that can splinter a healthy home. Written by a pastor who is a father of three grown sons and Benedictine Oblate of Mount Angel Abbey, this book includes dozens of practical suggestions and exercises based on the Benedictine monastic tradition.

978-0-8245-2524-8, paperback

Also by Elizabeth Ficocelli

Shower of Heavenly Roses
Stories of the Intercession of St. Thérèse of Lisieux

In times of joy, bereavement, and uncertainty, seekers of all
backgrounds have turned to Thérèse of Lisieux, the Little
Flower, asking her intercession for healing and guidance.
Shower of Heavenly Roses features the touching and
inspirational stories of dozens of men and women whose
petitions were answered with miracles large and small.
Whether you are struggling with a major life transition,
loss, and despair, or just looking to deepen your faith,
these stories will inspire you to a greater appreciation of
the power of prayer and miracles in our daily lives.

978-0-8245-2256-8 paperback

ABOUT THE AUTHOR

Elizabeth Ficocelli is a best-selling, award-winning author of fourteen books for adults and young people, including *Lourdes: Font of Faith, Hope & Charity; Shower of Heavenly Roses: Stories of the Intercession of St. Thérèse of Lisieux,* and *The Imitation of Christ for Children.* She has been published in numerous Catholic magazines such as *America, St. Anthony Messenger, Columbia Magazine, Catholic Parent,* and *Liguorian.* Elizabeth is a frequent guest on EWTN television programs as well as on Catholic radio. She is the host of *Answering The Call* on St. Gabriel Radio AM 820. Elizabeth has spoken at national Catholic conventions such as the L.A. Religious Education Congress and the National Catholic Educators Association Conference; state conferences such as the Indiana Catholic Women's Conference, Oklahoma City Catholic Women's Conference, Phoenix Catholic Women's Conference, and San Antonio Catholic Women's Conference; as well as at schools, parishes, and organizational meetings. For more information, please visit www.elizabethficocelli.com.